AF593234

Edited by DANNIE ABSE

POETRY DIMENSION 2

The Best of the Poetry Year

Robson Books

FIRST PUBLISHED IN HARDBACK IN GREAT BRITAIN IN 1974 BY ROBSON BOOKS LTD., 28 POLAND STREET, LONDON W1V 3DB. PUBLISHED SIMULTANEOUSLY IN PAPERBACK BY SPHERE BOOKS LTD

The publishers acknowledge with thanks the assistance of The Arts Council of Great Britain.

ISBN 0 903895 24 2

Printed in Great Britain by Hazell Watson & Viney Ltd
Aylesbury, Bucks

CONTENTS

Points of View

Poems from Magazines

Lives of the Poets

Introductory Note

This is the second anthology in a planned series of poetry annuals and, in compiling it, I have drawn mainly from periodicals, pamphlets and books published between and during the winter of 1973 and spring 1974 in England, Ireland, Scotland and Wales. I hope I have taken the best material from that time period and that readers will find this anthology not only enjoyable but will also be persuaded by the variousness and lucidity of British poetry and criticism being published now.

Acknowledgments are owed firstly to those authors who have allowed me to reprint their work; secondly to those editors and publishers named below the prose and poems printed in these pages. I should also like to thank Mr Jonathan Barker of the Poetry Library of the Arts Council of Great Britain for his aid and consideration.

D.A.

Criticism

Philip Larkin **It Couid Only Happen in England** [1]

The quickest way to start a punch-up between two British literary critics is to ask them what they think of the poems of Sir John Betjeman. For while their author has attained nearly every honour open to a writer of verse in his country, his work and its reputation still evoke a remarkable variety of response there.

Few at any rate would deny that the poems in this book make up the most extraordinary poetic output of our time. By extraordinary I don't necessarily mean good: good poems are surprising rather than extraordinary, keeping the power to inflict their tiny pristine shock long after they have become familiar; but good poems can seem extraordinary too at first (*Leaves of Grass*, 'The Wreck of the Deutschland'), and it is only when this extraordinariness wears off that we can see whether the surprise remains. One must admit first of all that Sir John (he was knighted in 1969) is an extraordinary man. He is not, as some might suppose, one of the landed gentry like Sir Osbert Sitwell, nor is he a member of some university, gallery or museum that provides him with a comfortable stipend. In fact his public image is that of a freelance television personality and literary journalist, the sort of person who crops up on cultural TV panel games ('Where's this? When was it built?' etc.), conducts the viewer round England's cathedrals or goes up in a balloon to point out vanished villages, and who can be relied on for an appropriate half-hour of reminiscence or anthology at Christmas. Somehow he manages to produce an occasional book, often heavily illustrated, on a topographical or architectural theme.

1. Written as an Introduction to the American edition of John Betjeman's enlarged *Collected Poems* published by Houghton Mifflin, Boston, and printed in Britain by The Cornhill Magazine.

But this is only half the story: Sir John is at once both a more and a less serious personality than this suggests. He is a Commander of the Order of the British Empire, a Companion of Literature, a Royal Fine Arts Commissioner, a governor of Pusey House, a holder of honorary doctorates from six universities. On the other hand, he is one of modern England's few upper-class licensed jesters: usually photographed roaring with laughter, he will ride a bicycle through crowded London, dress up in Henry James's morning clothes (which he seems to own), explain how much he still loves his old teddy-bear Archibald. How he finds time to write poems at all is a mystery: they certainly cannot take their origin in emotion recollected in tranquillity, for (to judge by appearances) Sir John has no tranquillity. His energy is boundless.

The many contradictions of this public role are sustained by a personal charm and enthusiasm remarkable in anyone, let alone a writer. Unaffected, self-deprecating, generously tolerant of the views of whoever he is speaking to (I remember once saying to him 'Churches arc all the same really', to which he replied 'Oh, I wouldn't say that', which on reflection seems the biggest understatement I have ever heard), he makes it hard for anyone to remain immune from the persuasive friendliness and honesty he radiates. Some critics, however, manage to do so, nor do they find Sir John's extraordinariness especially impressive. 'All right, suppose he does cavort round the country in a squashed hat and mackintosh, with his old teddy-bear under one arm and a copy of Crockford's *Clerical Directory* under the other, suppose he does write poems about Victorian gothic and sports girls and being afraid of death – the whole act is really only a hangover from those ghastly Twenties, isn't it? You remember, when everybody had to be "amusing" – owning pigeons and dyeing them pink and mauve, admiring people like Firbank and Angelica Kauffman, printing facetious rubbish on private presses and playing "practical jokes" that got in the way of people doing real work. Sure enough, he saw the red light – compare the typography of *Continual Dew* in 1937 with *Old Lights for New Chancels* in 1940 – but he didn't really do any more than turn himself into a woolly toy for what's left of the so-called upper classes, sucking up to the Royals and encouraging the bourgeois to snigger about saying "serviette" and poke fun at the Welfare State. Oh, it's been quite an achievement: when the rest of the boys are dead or creeping about in dark glasses like silver-haired mummies, Betjeman's got his K[1] and gold medal and all the rest of it – you've got to hand it to him. But it's the sort of thing that could only happen in England.'

American readers may like to judge the justice of this view.

'Betjeman has a mind of extraordinary originality; there is no one else remotely like him.' The speaker is Sir Maurice Bowra, as reported by the Earl of Birkenhead,[2] when both Birkenhead and Betjeman were Oxford undergraduates. The words have the ring of careful consideration, and came from a clever man: what can we infer from them? Not, at any rate, that Betjeman was a prize student: in fact he left Oxford without a degree. Nor, surely, that he was typical of his own or any other generation. What Bowra meant was that the sort of thing he heard this ex-Marlborough undergraduate say when he invited him to dinner in Wadham College was completely unlike the common talk of the day. Posterity can only conjecture what it was like: first, there was bound to be an astonishingly detailed

1. i.e. knighthood.
2. *John Betjeman's Collected Poems*, compiled and with an introduction by the Earl of Birkenhead (John Murray, 1958).

knowledge of church architecture, furnishing and monumental sculpture, nurtured by Betjeman's preparatory schoolmaster Gerald Haynes [1] mixed with a voluble brand of High Church camp about fiddleback chasubles and Eastern position and Low Church cocoa and so on. Then, a loving and vivid evocation of places, Cornwall, Highgate, the City of London; a gurgling celebration of little-known literature, the poems of the Reverend E. E. Bradford, the Reverend Robert Stephen Hawker, Campbell, and Arthur Machen's *The Secret Glory*; and over all a bubbling farcical affection, a self-abasing sense of ridicule, a defiant advocacy of the little, the obscure, the disregarded, all backed up with an astonishing memory and an outstanding gift for phrasing, not of the smart epigrammatic sort, but that which conjures a picture to fix whatever it is in the hearer's mind for ever. All this, coming from a toothy, somewhat baby-faced young man in a much too expensive suit and shirt and Charvet tie, was so unlike the general blague of the Twenties that the tough-minded Bowra knew he had picked a winner.

Betjeman was already in possession, at least in embryo, of the themes that were to make him famous, and they were resolutely opposed to the spirit of the century in two major ways: they were insular, and they were regressive. To compare Betjeman with a real figure of the Twenties, a Harold Acton, is to see immediately what a poor figure he would have cut in the Paris of Stein and Cocteau: he was not, and never has been, a cosmopolitan. To understand this we have to realise that at Betjeman's heart lies not poetry but architecture – or, if the concepts are allowed, a poetry that embraces architecture and an architecture that embraces poetry:

I only enjoy to the full the architecture of these

1. *See* John Betjeman: *Summoned by Bells* (John Murray, 1960), Ch. V.

islands. This is not because I am deliberately insular, but because there is so much I want to know about a community, its history, its class distinctions, and its literature, when looking at its buildings, that abroad I find myself frustrated by my ignorance. Looking at places is not for me just going to the church or the castle or the 'places of interest' mentioned in the guide book, but walking along the streets and lanes as well, just as in a country house I do not like to see state rooms only, but the passage to the billiard room, where the Spy cartoons are, and the bedrooms where I note the hairbrushes of the owner and the sort of hair-oil he uses. My hunt in a town is not just for one particular thing as an antiquary might look for Romanesque tympana, an art historian for a particular phase of baroque, or an architect for le Corbusier, but it is for the whole town . . . I like to see the railway station, the town hall, the suburbs, the shops, the signs of local crafts being carried on in backyards. I like to be able to know for certain where to place what I am looking at. In a building I like to be sure whether that building is an original or a very good fake. This I can do in my own country but am not so sure about in someone else's.[1]

And elsewhere, more emphatically:

For architecture means not a house, or a single building or a church, or Sir Herbert Baker, or the glass at Chartres, but your surroundings; not a town or a street, but our whole over-populated island.[2]

What Betjeman is saying here is that his fundamental interest is human life, or human life in

1. John Betjeman: *The English Town in the Last Hundred Years* (Cambridge Univ. Press, 1956), pp. 4–5.

2. John Betjeman: *Antiquarian Prejudice* (The Hogarth Press, 1939), p. 5.

society, and that architecture is important in human life because a good society is one dwelling in well-proportioned surroundings. This would seem to place him with writers such as Ruskin and Morris, people for whom the appearance of things approached a morality, and in a way this is true, for with Betjeman the eye leads the spirit: he tells us that he came to the Christian religion by means of church architecture and formal ritual. But Betjeman has always mocked Morris ('Hand-woven be my wefts, hand-made/My pottery for pottage'), and we shall see that it is not so much the architecture of a building that appeals to him as its relation to human use, to human scale and size, and the degree to which it reflects human life and emotions.

The quality of regressiveness I mentioned earlier might indeed be taken as no more than a latterday version of the anti-industrialism Morris and Ruskin and their followers so vehemently professed. If the spirit of our century is onwards, outwards and upwards, the spirit of Betjeman's work is backwards, inwards and downwards. If the architecture of our day is high-riser flats, its heroes the working class, its environment motorways lit with sodium, Betjeman exalts Comper interiors, clergymen's widows, and gaslight. If the age is agnostic and believes everyone is a socialist nowadays, Betjeman embraces the Christianity of the Church of England and proclaims a benevolent class system the best of all possible worlds. In a time of global concepts, Betjeman insists on the little, the forgotten, the unprofitable, the obscure; the privately-printed book of poems, the chapel behind the Corn Exchange, the local water-colours in the museum (open 2 p.m. to 4 p.m.). This, at any rate, is how the British public knows him: the man who is always trying to stop things being pulled down, or blocked in, or covered in wires or concrete railings or tarmac; the man who hates town clerks 'from north of Trent' and speculative builders, and all the modernisers and centralisers and rationalisers who are bent on making things easy for the motorist, or safe for the kiddies, or economic for the corporation cleansing department. To go for a drive with Betjeman is to enjoy a constant monologue on what he sees, a series of variations on the theme 'Gosh, how lovely' (interspersed, when he gets bored, with a flat voice that greets every fresh architectural prospect of distinction with the assurance 'We're 'avin' that down'); some idea of this may be gained from 'A Walk with Mr Betjeman', by Tom Driberg,[1] a fascinating and on the whole successful attempt to preserve a record of this highly-developed and humorous sensibility in action. Of course, Betjeman is not an isolated figure: there are many societies striving to preserve both town and countryside, and they are starting to link up with all who are increasingly concerned with the nature of our environment as the century nears its poisoned end, but Sir John is their figurehead, their most original voice, the signature that appears most often under letters to *The Times*. In fairness one should also point out that he got in first.

All this is a necessary prelude to an understanding of Betjeman's poems, partly because a great deal of what he writes is, overtly or covertly, propaganda for what he believes, partly because his poetic aesthetic is only another version of his social aesthetic. The first thing to realize about Betjeman as a writer of verse is that he is a poet for whom the modern poetic revolution has simply not taken place. Insularity and regression rule here as there. For him there has been no symbolism, no objective correlative, no T. S. Eliot or Ezra Pound, no reinvestment in myth or casting of language as gesture, no *Seven Types* or *Some Versions*, no works of criticism with titles such as *Communication as Discipline* or *Impli-*

1. *The New Statesman*, 6th January, 1961, pp. 9–10.

cit and Explicit Image-Obliquity in Sir Lewis Morris. He addresses himself to his art in the belief that poetry is an emotional business, and that rhyme and metre are means of enhancing that emotion, just as in the days when poetry was deemed a kind of supernatural possession (I have been trying, without much success, to think of any present-day work demanding such a hypothesis); the result is that Betjeman's poems, however trivial or light-hearted their subjects, always carry a kind of primitive vivacity that sets them apart from the verses ot his contemporaries and captures the reader's attention in advance of his intellectual consent:

Miss J. Hunter Dunn, Miss J. Hunter Dunn,
Furnish'd and burnish'd by Aldershot sun,
What strenuous singles we played after tea,
We in the tournament – you against me!

There lurks within him someone who weeps at Victorian ballads ('My heart finds rest, my heart finds rest in Thee') and roars out Edwardian comic songs ('There's something about a varsity man that distinguishes him from a cad'), someone to whom every poem seems to *matter* in a rare refreshing way. For Betjeman's poems, forthright, comprehensible, and couched in the marked button-holing rhythms of Praed or Tennyson, are nothing if they are not personal: they are exclusively about things that impress, amuse, excite, anger or attract him, and – and this is most important – once a subject has established its claim on his attention he never questions the legitimacy of his interest. Energy most contemporary poets put into screening their impulses for security Betjeman puts into the poem.

The result is, at first sight, a poetic corpus of extreme oddity: Betjeman, we remember, has a mind of extraordinary originality; there is no one else remotely like him. And yet his actual subjects, insofar as they are classifiable, are familiar enough:

topography, religion, satire, death, love and sex, people and childhood take care of four-fifths of the pieces, and really only an occasional poem is totally eccentric (for instance, 'The Heart of Thomas Hardy'). The uniqueness lies in his approach, a blend of the direct and the round-about. The verse just quoted is the opening of a love poem, yet what could be simultaneously more personal and ironic than the first line? The passionate reiteration of the beloved's name in a form in which it would appear, say, on her visiting-card conveys that she is clearly seen by the poet in the context of the middle classes, and that this increases her attraction for him. Betjeman has told us[1] that the poem was the expression of his feelings for a superintendent in the canteen of the Ministry of Information during the war, but even in such a traditionally direct exercise he has to invent the *persona* of a subaltern (or junior army officer), stage an imaginary (and somewhat masochistic) tennis match in Aldershot, and follow it with the most suburban of club dances. All this apparatus is necessary before he can say what he wishes to say – and yet, we reflect, Aldershot is a military town, and even if Betjeman was never a subaltern he did marry the daughter of a field-marshal: the poem's feeling is genuine, even if the properties are fiction – yet even the properties have, perhaps, a kind of truth.

Let us look more closely at a poem such as 'Middlesex': actually a lament for the disappearance of the countryside he knew as a boy because of the expansion of suburban London, it nevertheless starts with a gaily satiric portrait of 'fair Elaine the bobby-soxer' and a two-stanza description, acute but not unfriendly, of her home life. The subsequent switch to the River Brent may seem disconcerting, but a

1. *The Golden Treasury of John Betjeman* (Spoken Arts 710), Band 1. *See also The Sunday Times Magazine*, August 8, 1965, pp. 16–21.

rapid succession of rural cameos brings us (as so often) to the human element, the long-dead inhabitants of this long-lost peace, put forward under the names of minor characters from one of Betjeman's favourite books, George Grossmith's *The Diary of a Nobody*. Only then do we see fair Elaine's function, to contrast with these 'cockney anglers, cockney shooters' and represent, with her mindless consumption of branded products, those who now live in this built-over ex-paradise, her ironically Tennysonian name implying the decline such a transformation has entailed.

Transition to a more direct poem, 'The Metropolitan Railway', is easy, for past inhabitants of Ruislip are again the subject: a young Edwardian married couple ('your parents' – or his?) who come to London to work and shop respectively, and meet at Baker Street Station in the evening to go back together to 'autumn-scented Middlesex again'. In this case Betjeman first fixes our attention on a light-fitting of the period that remains in the station buffet the pair would have used: slowly he 'tracks' (the cinematic metaphor is almost inevitable) to the couple's arrival and day in Edwardian ('safe hydraulic lift') London; sharply the poem 'cuts' to the poignantly brutal:

Cancer has killed him. Heart is killing her.
  The trees are down. An Odeon flashes fire
Where stood their villa by the murmuring fir . . .

and its last line takes us back to the station buffet again with its hanging electrolier, the *art nouveau* of an age when 'Youth and Progress were in partnership', but now we see it with a new understanding of its place in the poem.

This kind of poetry (and I hope these few remarks have demonstrated, at least in outline, its existence and nature) has its parallel with Betjeman's kind of architecture: just as that meant 'our whole over-populated island', so the poetry means the furniture of our lives: 'The Metropolitan Railway' is about the lives of an Edwardian married couple, and by implication all married couples, but take away the early electric suburban railway, the period light-fitting, the 'sepia views of leafy lanes in Pinner', and the poem collapses. Betjeman is a true heir of Thomas Hardy, who found clouds, mists and mountains 'unimportant beside the wear on a threshold, or the print of a hand': his poems are about the threshold, but it and they would be nothing without the wear. 'For the landscape that most appeals to him,' as Mr John Sparrow wrote in his perceptive essay,[1] is the inhabited landscape: he cannot see a place without seeing also the life that is lived in it, without becoming conscious of its human associations . . . he can find matter for poetry in the least promising surroundings, provided they have an individual character and the breath of life.'

It isn't surprising, therefore, that his poems should be about people as well as places, nor that, just as places cannot be separated from people, so the people cannot be separated from their places. Each of them carries a sharply-realized background – Myfanwy and North Oxford, the clergyman's widow and the house of rest, the night-club proprietress deep in her frowsy London mews, business girls lying in rickety built-on bathrooms, even the church mouse among the long-discarded cassocks; through each of them we see a life we should never have known, in circumstances that may have already disappeared. Or, if they are not individuals, they still make up the element of humanity – the wear on the threshold – that is so essential in Betjeman's vision; the elderly Oxford dons in 'I. M. Walter Ramsden', and beyond them, like old rowing groups,

1. *Selected Poems by John Betjeman*, chosen with a preface by John Sparrow (John Murray, 1948).

the 'long-dead generations' going back beyond Ypres and the Somme to golden summers of Edward and Victoria:

> They remember, as the coffin to its final
>   obsequations
>   Leaves the gates,
> Buzz of bees in window boxes on their summer
>   ministrations,
>   Kitchen din,
>   Cups and plates,
> And the getting of bump suppers for the
>   long-dead generations
>   Coming in
>   From Eights.

Time and again, with Betjeman's best poems, the reader exclaims, But this is about a place! And then the realization follows that the place is presented in terms of its human association, without which it would be insignificant:

> . . . not a house, or a single building or a church
> . . . but your surroundings; not a town or a street,
> but our whole over-populated island.

Betjeman is consistent: he has said what he believes in, whether in architecture or poetry, and it is the backbone of his verse, at once its strength and its appeal. Of course it is not always imbued with compassion; sometimes it is tinged with fun – it would be a poor account of Betjeman that didn't say he is a master of the comic and the absurd – sometimes with amorousness, sometimes with satire: for someone often accused of tenderness towards the establishment, Betjeman spends an unusual amount of time attacking things, sometimes with quite remarkable ferocity ('Slough', 'In Westminster Abbey'). In such passages the social-history content of his verse rises sharply:

. . . the children have a motor-bus instead,
And in a town eleven miles away
We train them to be 'Citizens of Today'.
And many a cultivated hour they pass
In a fine school with walls of vita-glass.
Civics, eurhythmics, economics, Marx,
How-to-respect-wild-life-in-National-Parks;
Plastics, gymnastics – thus they learn to scorn
The old thatch'd cottages where they were born.
The girls, ambitious to begin their lives
Serving in WOOLWORTH's, rather than as wives;
The boys, who cannot yet escape the land,
At driving tractors lend a clumsy hand.
An eight-hour day for all, and more than three
Of these are occupied with making tea
And talking over what we all agree—
Though 'Music while you work' is now our wont,
It's not so nice as 'Music while you don't.'

It is customary to say that Betjeman fails as a satirist; he is certainly too kind a writer to be really savage. On the other hand, most literary critics these days are on the left wing, and so are unlikely to be appreciative of a passage such as the one above. For my part, I find the last five lines not only a pertinent summary of a subject no other present-day British poet has tried to deal with, but singularly unforgettable. But politics apart, his deceptively gentle verse can move into an attack so smooth its efficiency is seen only in retrospect:

Our lodging-house, ten minutes from the shore.
Still unprepared to make a picnic lunch
Except by notice on the previous day.
Still nowhere for the children when it's wet
Except that smelly, overcrowded lounge.
And still no garage for the motor-car.
Still on the bedroom wall, the list of rules:
Don't waste the water. It is pumped by hand.

Don't throw old blades into the W.C.
Don't keep the bathroom long and don't be late
For meals and don't hang swimsuits out on sills
(A line has been provided at the back).
Don't empty children's sand-shoes in the hall.
Don't this, Don't that. Ah, still the same, the same
As it was last year and the year before –
But rather more expensive now, of course.

But in fact Betjeman is an accepter, not a rejecter, of his time and the people he shares it with. The notion that he is a precious aesthete whose sensibilities are perpetually either quivering before Victoriana or shuddering at locutions such as 'toilet'[1] is totally misguided. On the contrary, he is a robust and responsive writer, registering 'Dear old, bloody old England' with vivacious precision and affectionate alliteration quite beyond most avowed social realists. His gusto embraces it all – the mouldy remnants of the nineteenth century, the appalling monoliths of the twentieth, the dead church, the dying peasantry, the conurbation and candy-floss and King's College, Cambridge – all the sadness and silliness and snobbery is potential Betjeman material. I have sometimes thought that this collection of Betjeman's poems would be something I should want to take with me if I were a soldier leaving England: I can't think of any other poet who has preserved so much of what I should want to remember, nor one who, to use his own words, would so easily suggest 'It is those we are fighting for, foremost of all.' This may not be an orthodox critical judgement, but I don't see why it shouldn't be taken into account.

I have every sympathy with the American reader faced with the task of arbiting on the value of these poems. To start with, Betjeman constitutes a kind of

1. E.g. 'Are the requisites all in the toilet?' Perhaps the American equivalent would be 'bathroom'.

distorting mirror in which all our critical catch-phrases appear in gross unacceptable parody. He is *committed*, *ambiguous*, and *ironic*; he is *conscious of literary tradition* (but quotes the wrong authors); he is a *satirist* (but on the wrong side); he has his own *White Goddess* (in blazer and shorts). And he has done all those things such as *forging a personal utterance*, *creating a private myth*, *bringing a new language and new properties to poetry*, and even (more than a hundred thousand copies of the first edition of his *Collected Poems* were sold) *giving back poetry to the general reader*, all equally undeniably, yet none of them in quite the way we meant. No wonder our keen critical tools twitch fretfully at his approach.

From this point of view alone he represents a worthwhile challenge to readers of any country. I can well imagine the American demurring, however, on the grounds that Betjeman is like cricket, something absolutely peculiar to these islands and in consequence absolutely unexportable. 'All these place names and English products – Ruislip Gardens (how d'you pronounce Ruislip?), Windsmoor, Jacqmar, Drene, Innoxa, Brent, Wembley, Northolt . . . and what's this *bona fide* stuff? And this cockney (what's that?) book I haven't read: you've told me what it is, but he doesn't . . . No, I'm sorry, this is just too private for me. I don't mind how many local cracks he puts in, that's his privilege, but he'll have to take the consequences.' Such an attitude would be understandable, but there are several points to be made in reply. First, and perhaps rather unexpectedly, an English reader would go some of the way with it. I know Brent, Wembley, Northolt and so on are in Middlesex, because Betjeman tells me so, but I've never been there and what I feel about them depends entirely on what he tells me about them: they might as well be in New York State. In 'The Metropolitan Railway' the same applies to all the place-names; I don't know what the Bromsgrove Guild was (though I can guess), and I don't know where the quotation comes from in the last stanza. Some of Betjeman's poems ar^ completely incomprehensible to me (e.g. 'The Irish Unionist's Farewell to Greta Hellstrom in 1922') while remaining emotionally potent. In sum, the English reader is going to need an annotated Betjeman almost as soon as the American.

Secondly, it isn't outrageously novel to expect a little topographical and period background to a work of literature on the part of its reader: think of James Joyce's Dublin. The crucial point is whether the reader gets enough out of the work initially to make it worth his while solving the references to deepen his enjoyment. In the case of Betjeman there are enough universal situations ('Cancer has killed him. Heart is killing her') to make this so; at a lighter level, there is enough fun to be had from the rhymes and metres. The task would be similar to, say, picking up the Regency references ('And boroughs were bought without a test') in Winthrop Mackworth Praed.

Even if I have been under-estimating the American reader, however, he still might say something like 'All right, so Betjeman's English like Joyce is Irish, but even so I can't believe these poems add up to much: places get described, and there are a few sketches of people (mostly ones it's too bad about), and some pretty good evocations of the past, *eheu fugaces* and all that, and some comedy, but all in all it seems minor to me. What are you ranking it with? Eliot? Auden? Honestly I don't think it makes that grade. It's more like what you were saying, you know, Twenties stuff, Bright Young Things and so on. Not serious.' Well, in a sense this is where we started: this is where the punch-ups begin in England.

Betjeman is serious because he has produced an original poetry of persons and surroundings in which neither predominates: each sustains the other, and the poetry is in the sustaining. His texture is subtle, a constant flickering between solemn and comic, self-mockery and self-expression; to compare him (again) with Praed brings out the mechanical side of the latter, and the essentially *vers de société* quality of his switches of feeling. To compare him with Housman or Hopkins tempts one to talk in terms of poetic ballistics: they penetrate deeper, but he makes a bigger hole, by which I mean only that while I doubt if any of Betjeman's pieces can be advanced against 'Tell me not here', or 'I wake, and feel the fell of dark' (still less 'The Wreck of the Deutschland'), he can claim a much greater range of theme and manner and metre. He offers us, indeed, something we cannot find in any other writer – a gaiety, a sense of the ridiculous, an affection for human beings and how and where they live, a vivid and vivacious portrait of mid-twentieth century English social life.

To say he is unique, however ('there is no one else remotely like him'), is not to say that he stands outside the course of poetic history. I once wrote that Betjeman was 'one of the rare figures on whom the aesthetic appetites of an age pivot and swing round to face an entirely new direction':[1] certainly it is worth noting that, forty years after he began to publish, young men are bearded like Victorian paterfamilias and young ladies are draped in *art nouveau* shifts. But it applies to poetry as well. I have already said that he has little in common with what we call 'modern' poetry; his remarkable popularity in England is partly due to this. For it is as obvious as it is strenuously denied that in this century English poetry went off on a loop-line that took it away from the general reader. Several factors caused this. One was the aberration of modernism, that blighted all the arts. One was the emergence of English literature

1. *Listen*, Vol. III. No. 2 (Spring, 1959), p. 14.

as an academic subject, and the consequent demand for a kind of poetry that needed elucidation. One, I am afraid, was the culture-mongering activities of the Americans Eliot and Pound. In any case, the strong connection between poetry and the reading public that had been forged by Kipling, Housman, Brooke and *Omar Khayaam* was destroyed as a result. It is arguable that Betjeman was the writer who knocked over the 'No Road Through to Real Life' signs that this new tradition had erected, and who restored direct intelligible communication to poetry, not as a pompous pseudo-military operation of literary warfare but simply by exclaiming 'Gosh, how lovely' (or 'Gosh, how awful') and roaring with laughter. He became the living contradiction of Eliot's contention that the better the poet, the more complete the separation between the man who suffers and the man who creates.

His relation to Eliot is in fact curious. One of the more striking passages in *Summoned by Bells* describes how, as a schoolboy in Highgate, he fancied his poems were 'as good as Campbell now':

> And so I bound my verse into a book
> *The Best of Betjeman*, and handed it
> To one who, I was told, liked poetry –
> The American master, Mr Eliot.

Thc scene is worthy of a nineteenth-century narrative painter: 'The Infant Betjeman Offers His Verses To The Young Eliot'. For, leaving aside the question of their respective poetic statures, it was Eliot who gave the modernist poetic movement its charter in the sentence 'Poets in our civilization, as it exists at present, must be difficult',[1] and it was Betjeman who was to by-pass the whole light industry of critical exegesis that had grown up round this fatal phrase by demonstrating that a direct

1. T. S. Eliot: *Selected Essays*, 3rd ed. (Faber, 1951), p. 289.

relation with the reading public could be established by anyone able to be moving and memorable.

This sounds as if the two were in opposition, but I am not sure that Betjeman has not a strong affinity to 'the American master'. Why must poets be 'difficult'? Because 'our civilization comprehends great variety and complexity, and this variety and complexity, playing upon a refined sensibility, must produce various and complex results'.[1] Why should a poet bother himself with this complexity? Because:

> there is an aspect in which we can see religion as the *whole way of life* ot a people, from birth to the grave, from morning to night and even in sleep, and that way of life is also its culture.[2]

And what is this 'whole way of life' that a poet should (presumably) concern himself with expressing? Eliot was obliging enough to leave us a list of its properties:

> Derby Day, Henley Regatta, Cowes, the twelfth of August, a cup final, the dog races, the pin table, the dart board, Wensleydale cheese, boiled cabbage cut in sections, beetroot in vinegar, nineteenth century gothic churches, and the music of Elgar.[3]

Now if this passage reminds us of anyone's poetry, it is Betjeman's rather than Eliot's or anyone else's. But over and above this, what kind of response is Eliot adumbrating, if not the one I have already quoted from Betjeman?

> . . . how much is embraced by the word culture. It includes all the characteristic activities and interests of a people.[4]

1. T. S. Eliot: *Selected Essays*, 3rd ed. (Faber, 1951).
2. T. S. Eliot: *Notes Towards the Definition of Culture* (Faber, 1948), p. 31.
3. *Ibid.*
4. *Ibid.*

> . . . not a house, or a single building or a church . . . but your surroundings; not a town or street, but your whole over-populated island.

It is, to say the least of it, notable that both writers should have chosen to emphasize the identical element of cultural inclusiveness in describing what they most value; perhaps it is a coincidence, like the fact that both of them, by their different ways, were led to Anglicanism and the Church of England. It does, however, provide another instance of Betjeman fulfilling one of our critical criteria in an unexpected and not entirely acceptable way. Can it be that, as Eliot dominated the first half of the twentieth century, the second half will derive from Betjeman? I do not think this is as completely unlikely a suggestion as it might first appear. After all, he may be unique, but he is not solitary. Behind him stand Hardy, Tennyson, Crabbe, Cowper, the Reverend Robert Stephen Hawker – all those on whom he descanted so persuasively at Sir Maurice Bowra's dinner table many years ago.

The Cornhill Magazine

Elizabeth Bishop was quoted triumphantly on the dust jacket of the 1969 *Notebook*: 'Somehow or other, by fair means or foul, and in the middle of our worst century so far, we have produced a magnificent poet.' I feel no need to demur, though strictly I've no right to an opinion, being British and so no part of that 'we', that 'our'. Plenty of people must have felt, though, as the original *Notebook* of May 1969 was already changed in July of that year and radically changed as well as expanded for the London edition of 1970, that the Lowell verse-machine was not just overheating but also throwing up ever more sludge and waste. In a poem at the end of one of his new books, *History*, Lowell quotes somebody, perhaps himself, on his own career:

> surviving to dissipate *Lord Weary's Castle*
> and nine subsequent useful poems
> in the seedy grandiloquence of *Notebook*.

But the fact that the poet has anticipated an objection shouldn't stop us from raising it, if we think it just. And in fact something of the kind is unavoidable once we realize that of the three new books, two once again announce themselves as quarried out of *Notebook*. What sort of game is this poet playing with his public – apart, of course, from making money out of us? How resist the suspicion that *Notebook*, at least in its first version, if not indeed in its second and third, was just an unconsidered emptying out on to the page of every scribble and doodle that Lowell had perpetrated over several years? Of *History* Lowell says: 'About 80 of the poems . . . are new, the rest are taken from my last published poem, *Notebook* . . . All the poems have been changed, some heavily. I have plotted. My old title, *Notebook*, was more accurate than I wished; i.e., my composition was jumbled. I hope this jumble or jungle is cleared – that I have cut the waste marble from the figure.' Fair enough. But 'plot' was already being claimed for *Notebook* in its first version: 'My plot rolls with the seasons,' he said then. And when we discover that the 370 poems of *History* are mostly arranged in the simple chronological order of the dates at which their overt subjects (Alexander, Caligula, Mary Stuart, Lincoln, etc.) appeared on the stage of history, we cannot but think that the Michelangelesque metaphor about the waste marble being cut away from the figure is indeed grandiloquent, and that it promises a lot more than is performed. Can we call it plotting, let alone 'sculpture', when all the poet has done is sort his poems into loose categories merely by subject matter?

However, this is unfair. There is indeed sculpturesque energy of a very imperious and exciting sort when we find 3 sonnets (out of 4) in *Notebook* under the heading 'Searchings', compressed into one called 'Statue of Liberty':

> I like you like trees . . . you make me lift my eyes –
> the treasonable bulge behind your iron toga,
> the thrilling, chilling silver of your laugh,
> the hysterical digging of your accursed spur,
> Amazon, gazing on me, pop-eyed, cool,
> ageless, not holding back your war-whoop – no
>   chicken
> still game for swimming bare-ass with the boys.
> You catch the frenetic spotlight we sling about
> your lighthouse promontory, flights an inch
> from combustion and the drab of ash . . .
> While youth lasts your flesh is never fallen –
> high above our perishable flesh,
> the icy foam rubber waterfall stands firm
> metal pear-pointing to eternity.

The first line is from one sonnet, lines 3 to 7 are from another, lines 8 and 9 and also lines 10 to 14, (adapted), from yet another. Moreover, the original poems all belonged to private life, whereas the new poem is public (though with valuable private resonances – the statue is American womanhood as well as Liberty). Also, we pick up a thread of plot, since 'Statue of Liberty' follows a sonnet, much revised from a quite different place in *Notebook*, about walking in pinching shoes in Buenos Aires:

> the Republican martyrs lie in Roman temples;
> marble goddesses calm each Liberal hero
> still pale from the great kiss of Liberty . . .
> All night till my shoes were bloody – I found rest
> cupping my soft palm to her stone breast.

Though the strain of the adaptation shows through, for instance in the musical shapelessness of line 6, still this is an impressive example of the merely anecdotal purged and lifted to a new power. The anecdotal should not have been published in the first place; but let that pass. (What happened, by the way, to the practice of indexing books of poems alphabetically by titles and first lines? Neither Faber nor Farrar, Straus do us this courtesy, though these books cry out for it urgently.)

In any case, each edition of *Notebook* carried a clear warning that in Lowell's usage, 'plot' was an unusually capacious notion: 'Single poems and sections are opportunist and inspired by impulse. Accident threw up subjects, and the plot swallowed them – famished for human chances.' And a sonnet for Berryman that survives through both *Notebooks* into *History* makes the same point:

> John, we used the language as if we made it.
> Luck threw up the coin, and the plot swallowed,
> monster yawning for its mess of pottage.

Which enables us, leaving all sorts of questions unanswered, at least to begin answering one question we've posed already: what sort of game Lowell is playing with us. We can begin by saying that it's an exceptionally *intimate* game: we are to be with him, we *have* to be with him, as he runs a distracted hand through his hair, leafing through his old files and trying to see what his recent writing amounts to; where and how, if at all, it 'adds up'. As much with *History* as with any of the *Notebooks* we are really left to do the adding up for ourselves – *if we can*, the poet himself having virtually admitted that for his part he can't. And so, for 'intimate' in this sense we might as well read 'democratic'. From that demotic idiom which has become, since Williams, ever more *de rigueur* for American poets, Lowell is excluded because of his early schooling in the drumming decasyllable, 'the mighty line'; his coquettish habits of publishing are his way of achieving by other means a sort of unbuttoned welcome of the reader in the workshop, something that other American poets have achieved through a low-key idiom that he's debarred from.

All the same, 'coquettish' is an abusive word, and it has to be. For as readers we just don't know where we are, or what is expected of us. For instance, if from one point of view these procedures are democratic, in another light they are just the opposite, for the poems seem to come to us under the lordly rubric, 'Never apologize, never explain.' The whole collection, *For Lizzie and Harriet*, appears to assume that we know about Lowell's marital arrangements and how they've changed lately. If we don't know about this, we don't know where to go for information; and we feel like people absentmindedly invited to a party where everyone else is in the know and knows everyone else. The least we might expect is to be introduced to at least one other person in the room; and in his 'Afterthought' to the 1970 London

Notebook, Lowell did that much, explaining the poem that stood first in *Notebook* and that now stands first in *For Lizzie and Harriet*:

Half a year, then a year and a half, then
ten and a half – the pathos of a child's fractions,
  turn-
ing up each summer. God a seaslug. God a queen
with forty servants, God . . . she gave up – things
  whirl
in the chainsaw bite of whatever squares
the universe by name and number. For
the hundredth time, I slice through fog, and round
the village with my headlights on the ground,
as if I were the first philosopher,
as if I were trying to pick up a car
key . . . It can't be here, and so it must be there
behind the next crook in the road or growth
of fog – there blinded by our feeble beams,
of face, clock-white, still friendly to the earth.

Of these lines, which he said were 'as hermetic as any in the book', Lowell wrote in 1970: 'The "fractions" mean that my daughter, born in January, is each July, a precision important to a child, something and a half years old. The "Seaslug etc." are her declining conceptions of God.' With this note to help, we can admire the order of ideas and images through the poem, in particular the propriety by which the moon, measure of time, in the end escapes 'name and number' by being pointed to only in a riddling circumlocution. But in *For Lizzie and Harriet*, there is no note and all we are given instead is the child's birthdate: 'January 4, 1957'. Moreover the new version gives, for lines 9–11,

Like the first philosopher Thales who thought all
  things water,
and fell in a well . . . trying to find a car
key . . . It can't be here, and so it must be there

– which switches the whole thing on to a track of frigidly playful pedantry.

What I've been saying smacks fustily of those rightly suspect arguments, once so common in America and still to be heard in England, which begin: 'The reader has his rights also . . .' The trouble with this is that it presupposes certain assumptions, shared by the poet and his public, about what poetry is or what it does. And the truth is, on the contrary, that even less than his readers is the poet nowadays (a poet such as Lowell) clear about what he is doing, and why. In those circumstances, it might be said, the only honest thing for him to do is to let it come, let it tumble out, pell-mell – in hopes that some one, somewhere, will discern the design and the purpose that escape him. If he still talks incongruously about cutting away the waste marble, we need only suppose that he's less good at writing blurbs than at writing poems. However, this doesn't explain how he can still revise. For if he doesn't know what he is doing, or why, how can he decide that one set of words suits his purpose better than another? And in any case, such decisions crop up at every moment in composition as in revision: the puerile enjambement, 'turn/ing' – why did Lowell perpetrate it in the first place, and then adhere to it when he came to revise? He must have had *some* reason; can we believe it was the sort of thing that dazzles the freshman writing seminar, a disposition of line-endings so as to (get it?) *enact* the turning that it talks about? Such odds and ends of reach-me-down 'technique' are quite worthless in the absence of any conviction about the point of the poetic enterprise as a whole. One takes the point easily enough that he's sick of the well-made poem, the expensive art object, as an end in itself; but if that is thrown out the door, along with it have to go related fantasies about 'enactment'. And no amount of coquettish publishing can mask, or make up for, directionless composing.

However, for the poet who has lost direction (or deliberately abjured it, as Lowell for honorable reasons seems to have abjured the prophetic and denunciatory direction of *Near the Ocean*, for instance), another option is open: he can bring it about that the life he lives brings him into situations at once extreme and typical, in such a way that poems skimmed off that life, though they have in themselves no more direction than entries in a journal, feed upon and take over the direction that the life has. And this seems to be the case with *The Dolphin*, much the best of these three collections and the one that owes next to nothing to *Notebook*. On extreme and typical situation here is that of exile, the self-sought exile of Lowell in England which naturally and inevitably becomes for him the paradigm of exile in general;

> Is it honorable for a Jew to die as a Jew?
> Even the German officials encouraged Freud
> to go to Paris where at least he was known;
> but what does it matter to have a following,
> if no one, not even the concierge, says *good day*?
> He took a house in London's amused humdrum
> to prove that Moses must have been Egyptian –
> 'What is more monstrous than outliving your
>   body?'
> What do we care for the great man of culture –
> Freud's relations were liquidated at Belsen,
> Moses Cohn who had nothing to offer culture
> was liquidated at Belsen. Must we die,
> living in places we have learned to live in,
> completing the only work we're trained to do?

'London's amused humdrum' is brilliantly just and caustic, to characterize the peculiarly English brand of philistinism; and it may serve, as well as any of dozens of equally quotable throw-aways, to show how the marmoreal conclusiveness of the mighty line survives into Lowell's most recent writing, even now when pentameter and sonnet alike are consistently violated and, as it were, disembowelled. In fact, part of the superiority of *The Dolphin* to *For Lizzie and Harriet* can be seen in the readiness of the later poem to stay with the iambic pentameter quite comfortably for several lines at a time; the compulsion to disrupt it, at whatever cost in arbitrary ugliness, seems to be something that Lowell has for the moment worked out of his system.

All the same, *The Dolphin* stays within the framework of *Notebook* and the poems that came out of *Notebook*, to the extent that 'Lizzie' and 'Caroline' and 'Harriet' are characters in a drama we're supposed to know about. And in fact *The Dolphin* pushes intimacy to a new extreme; of poems like 'In the Mail' or 'Exorcism' or 'Foxfur' the first thing to say is that they are acutely embarrassing. Or so any one will feel who remembers, perhaps wistfully, the proprieties that went without saying up to 20 years ago. It was Lowell's own *Life Studies* that put an end to such automatic reticences; and the course which he then adopted, of making public what had been thought to be inviolably private, is the course that he sails on still. The privacies which he betrays are for the most part not those of the bedroom, but of the living room, the telephone booth, the mailbox. To my mind this makes them no less shocking, for I agree with George Steiner that fornication and buggery on stage and screen are alarming not because they expose sexuality, but because they expose *privacy*. The right to privacy for one's self, and the right not to look when the privacies of others are exposed, are rights that are now derided, if not yet explicitly denied. And for this surely baleful development, Lowell has to take some of the blame.

And yet there's no reason to think him a compulsive exhibitionist. He could have come to this practice by a line of argument which does him credit. For indeed everything I've noticed so far – Lowell's ways of publishing no less than his ways of writing (style as well as subject) – make sense only if we see them as one more desperate phase in the struggle, waged ever since the Romantics, to cut poetry clear of rhetoric. According to the Romantics' logic, as soon as the poet looks outside the circle of his intimates, and thinks of his public (of an anonymous third party – to be interested and intrigued, in short, to be *persuaded*), he is operating no longer as poet but as rhetorician. And Lowell, because he has been famous for so long, has to go to desperate lengths so as not to write with his avidly interested public in mind. He can do this (so I guess) only by writing much and writing fast – by, as it were, jumping himself into each poem; also by cramming into the poem things that will be meaningful only to his intimates; also by refusing to distinguish between the private and the public. It is a real bind for him; and his struggles in it, from *Notebook* onward, are heroic. But of course the facts of his situation, if he can suppress them from his mind as he writes, catch up with him unavoidably when he publishes. At that point it becomes impossible to pretend any longer that the faceless public doesn't exist. Writing poems may or may not be a rhetorical operation (I believe it is, in part, and has to be), but certainly publishing them is. And so long as Lowell continues to publish, his struggles not to be a rhetorician, though they may be heroic, are certainly in the last analysis fatuous.

Fortunately, by the time he finished *The Dolphin* – perhaps before he started it, certainly by the time he passed it for publication – Lowell had reached these conclusions for himself. He has had the grace to allow that the poems which present themselves as literal transcripts of letters and phone calls may be nothing of the kind (I am devoutly glad to hear it, and over-ready to believe him); he has by implication taken the side of the arch-rhetorician Yeats: and he has 'plotted' the book in an acceptable public sense, by way of a cluster of dominant images signalized by the title – images of fishnets, stirred mud, eels, salmon-trout. When he says,

> After fifty so much joy has come,
> I hardly want to hide my nakedness—
> the shine and stiffness of a new suit, a feeling,
> not wholly happy, of being reborn,

he seems to be referring in the first place to his new marriage and his new child; but his public, which is interested in *public* meanings, comes across enough evidence that the new life is a new life of his art also, a shucking off at last of the self-contradictions that snarled him in *Notebook* and the collections that came out of *Notebook*. In this new dispensation, if it's still true that 'Everything is real until it's published' – why, that's just the name of the game, the shadow of the rhetorician's dishonesty that necessarily falls on all of us who 'go on typing to go on living.'

Parnassus

A. Walton Litz **The Waste Land, Fifty Years After**

The fiftieth anniversary of the publication of T. S. Eliot's *The Waste Land* was an obvious occasion for critical revaluation. Already we are separated from the great works of that *annus mirabilis*, 1922, by a distance in time and sensibility as great as that which separated Eliot and Pound and Joyce from their Victorian predecessors. In the late 1940's, when I first encountered *The Waste Land*, I could still read Eliot as if he were my contemporary: evidence both of the extraordinary impact of the 'modernist' movement and of *The Waste Land*'s central place in that movement. Few works can have remained *avant-garde* for so long. But now that 'modernism' has passed into the realm of literary history *The Waste Land* must pass with it, helped on its way by the recent discovery and publication of the original manuscripts and typescripts. *The Waste Land* and Eliot's other poems will never look quite the same again.

To me *The Waste Land* has always been the classic example of the 'really new' work of art, as Eliot himself describes it in 'Tradition and the Individual Talent': the radical achievement which enters the established order of literary works and causes a permanent shift in our perspective, so that the entire idea of a literary tradition is significantly altered. This position of *The Waste Land* as the central or normative statement of a new literary age was recognized from the start. In July 1922, three months before the poem's publication, Ezra Pound wrote to his former teacher Felix E. Schelling that 'Eliot's *Waste Land* is I think the justification of the "movement," of our modern experiment, since 1900.' Like Joyce's *Ulysses*, *The Waste Land* was acknowledged as a revolutionary document while still a work in progress. It was part of the propaganda, as well as the crowning achievement, of the 'new poetry' of 1909–1922.

A moment ago I referred to my own first reading of Eliot as an encounter with a 'contemporary': I suspect that mine was the last generation which could confront him on that particular ground. The experience of *The Waste Land* as a contemporary poem now belongs to literary history, although – interestingly enough – the same cannot be said for that other master-document of 1922, Joyce's *Ulysses*. As Richard Ellmann remarks in the opening sentence of his great biography, 'We are still learning to be James Joyce's contemporaries,' and all the criticism of this anniversary year seems to bear him out. The burden of the recent conferences, reviews, and articles has been that we are still learning to read *Ulysses*, whereas in the case of Eliot the time has come for 'revaluation' and placing. Whether we believe that Eliot was the Arnold of his age, or prehaps the Cowley, the time for such judgments *has* come.

The facsimile publication of Eliot's drafts and revisions for *The Waste Land* has done more than reveal the latent possibilities in the finished poem: it has made us all aware of the critical slogans and textbook schemas which produced, over the past twenty-five years, a 'standard' interpretation of *The Waste Land* that has coloured our view of Eliot's entire achievement. Most critics of the poem – lured by its surface complexity and the intriguing notes – have treated *The Waste Land* as a sacred text in need of an ordinary gloss, thus delivering a critical model more orderly, more 'traditional,' and more moralistic than the poem itself. And this standard or normative reading of *The Waste Land* has, in turn, distorted our understanding of the later poetry and drama.

The first cause of this distorting process appears to have been Eliot's well-known review of Joyce's

Ulysses ('*Ulysses*, Order, and Myth', published in *The Dial* in November 1923), which was taken to mean that Eliot and Joyce had employed the same 'mythical method'. Here is the crucial passage in Eliot's essay:

'In using the myth, in manipulating a continuous parallel between contemporaneity and antiquity, Mr. Joyce is pursuing a method which others must pursue after him. They will not be imitators, any more than the scientist who uses the discoveries of an Einstein in pursuing his own, independent, further investigations. It is simply a way of controlling, of ordering, of giving a shape and a significance to the immense panorama of futility and anarchy which is contemporary history . . . It is a method for which the horoscope is auspicious. Psychology (such as it is, and whether our reaction to it be comic or serious), ethnology, and *The Golden Bough* have concurred to make possible what was impossible even a few years ago. Instead of narrative method, we may now use the mythical method. It is, I seriously believe, a step toward making the modern world possible for art . . .'

The implications of this passage would seem to be quite clear. As Thomas Mann once said, the task of the modern artist is to convert the individual and the bourgeois into the typical and the mythical, and *Ulysses* showed Eliot one way to accomplish such a transformation. As assistant editor of the *Egoist* and close reader of the *Little Review*, the magazines in which the early chapters of *Ulysses* appeared serially, Eliot would have been familiar with Joyce's use of myth by late 1919; and the delicate exchanges between past and present in *The Waste Land* obviously owe a great deal to Joyce's method. Nonetheless, there are sharp differences between the use of the *Odyssey* in *Ulysses* and the use of the Grail legend in *The Waste Land*, differences that are often overlooked. They are brought into focus by

Eliot's comment that the mythical method can be used as a substitute for the effects of conventional narration. In Joyce's novel the *Odyssey* provides an hypothetical or ideal plot as well as a fixed standard of human psychology, a plot that parallels or counterpoints the contemporary action; but the Grail legend, as retold by Jessie Weston, supplies not a plot but a structure of values (or, if you will, a ritualistic norm). In treating Eliot's use of the Grail legend as if it were analogous to Joyce's use of the *Odyssey*, many critics have supplied *The Waste Land* with a spurious plot which exists outside the poem, and which fosters the mistaken notion that *The Waste Land* (like a five-act tragedy) moves from conflict through reversal into some sort of resolution. What is essentially an internal drama is turned by this method into an external quest whose outcome can only be fragmentary or inconclusive. In sum, the leading critics of the poem have too often produced a temporal rather than a spatial pattern, and have discerned a set of moralistic judgments on life where nothing was intended but a delicate balance of attitudes. Just as the early defenders of *Ulysses* overemphasized the novel's mechanical orders as a defense against philistine charges of 'formlessness' or 'chaotic construction', so the early admirers of *The Waste Land* were determined to give every line a moral meaning in order to rescue Eliot from charges of negativism and nihilism. The result has too often been a programmatic interpretation that makes *The Waste Land* seem little different from the ironic Sweeney poems or 'Burbank with a Baedeker'. Much might be gained if readers ot *The Waste Land* could, for a few years, adopt the motto Mark Twain affixed to *Huckleberry Finn*: 'persons attempting to find a moral in [this work] will be banished; persons attempting to find a plot in it will be shot'.

It would be my contention that the essential life of *The Waste Land* does not lie in the obvious contrasts between past and present which inform most of the set pieces. The famous description of the modern woman at her dressing table ('The Chair she sat in, like a burnished throne,/Glowed on the marble . . .') is less interesting for what it tells us about Cleopatra and her modern counterpart than for what we learn about Eliot's conception of heroic verse. Nor does the quick of the poem lie in the broad thematic contrasts between two kinds of life and two kinds of death, the dual symbolisms of fire and water. If this were so, *The Waste Land* would be fit only for courses on religious ideas in literature. *The Waste Land* is not *about* spiritual dryness, it is about the ways in which that dryness can be perceived and expressed. Like Ezra Pound's *Hugh Selwyn Mauberley*, it is a museum of verse forms, an experiment with language, the record of a special sensibility exposed to the anxieties of a particular culture. Perhaps it would be best if we refrained, at least for a little while, from thinking of *The Waste Land* as a major revelation of modern man's spiritual plight – 'an *Inferno* which looked towards a *Purgatorio*' – and thought of it as a master document of the modernist movement in literature, a work that both culminates the movement and performs an act of criticism upon it.

Once freed from its burden of spiritual significance, the poem can then be approached in a variety of ways, and with more humour and tact than it has usually received. The satiric turns in the manner of Pound's verses on contemporary manners; the parodies and ventriloquial effects of the English music hall; the oblique comments on the foreground of English poetry; the persistent strain of Augustan irony; the combination of a precise topography with a dream landscape; the vindication of poetry as ritual and mystery; the violent yoking of realism and surrealism; literary variations on the effects of collage Cubism; montage techniques borrowed from the repertoire of the early cinema – these aspects and many more would have to be explored in any analysis of *The Waste Land* that aimed at balance and completeness. The question is really one of where to begin, and what to emphasize. So as one step toward establishing critical priorities, I would like to take up the vexed question of the notes to the poem and Eliot's use of 'sources', topics that lead directly to a consideration of how *The Waste Land* achieved its present unity of form in the months of late 1921 and early 1922.

When *The Waste Land* was first published in magazine form in the autumn of 1922 it was free of annotation: the notes to the poem were added – according to Ezra Pound – at the express wish of the first book publisher, Liveright, who 'wanted a longer volume and the notes were the only available unpublished matter'. Evidently Eliot's attitude toward the entire apparatus of references and sources, like that of most of his readers, was ambiguous from the start. The fundamental notes were never, of course, a hoax or a publisher's gimmick; they existed in private form during the writing of the poem, and were used by Eliot's friends as *The Waste Land* circulated in typescript. In this sense, the original notes were an integral part of the poem, not unlike the elaborate chart of symbolic correspondences and Homeric parallels that Joyce circulated privately for the benefit of the first readers of *Ulysses*. It is interesting and revealing that these two great monuments of the modernist movement, published in the same year, should have come into the world trailing their own guides to interpretation. Obviously, Joyce's *schema* and Eliot's notes were part of the 'cultic' atmosphere that surrounded both writers. They were the top-secret information needed for any successful revolution; they flaunt the fact that modern literature must be intricate and difficult, that it involves hard intellectual effort, and that for a time it must be nurtured by a coterie of those who know. So at bottom, Eliot's later regrets that the notes were so widely circulated have nothing to do with the validity of the notes themselves, but rather with their effect on the general audience once they escaped the hands of the initiated. Like Joyce's *schema*, once it was revealed by Stuart Gilbert, the notes had a centrifugal effect on most criticism, driving the reader away from the work and into ever-widening circles of source-study and influence-charting.

In his 1956 lecture on 'The Frontiers of Criticism' (later published in *On Poetry and Poets*) Eliot made his best-known comment on the notes, a comment remarkable both for its distortion of the original circumstances and for its implication that only the critics have been led into temptation, while the initiated – Eliot's fellow poets – have known how to handle the information.

'Here I must admit that I am, on one conspicuous occasion, not guiltless of having led critics into temptation. The notes to *The Waste Land*! I had at first intended only to put down all the references for my quotations, with a view to spiking the guns of critics of my earlier poems who had accused me of plagiarism. Then, when it came to print *The Waste Land* as a little book – for the poem on its first appearance in *The Dial* and in *The Criterion* had no notes whatever – it was discovered that the poem was inconveniently short, so I set to work to expand the notes, in order to provide a few more pages of printed matter, with the result that they became the remarkable exposition of bogus scholarship that is still on view today. I have sometimes thought of getting rid of these notes; but now they can never be unstuck. They have had almost greater popularity than the poem itself – anyone who bought my book of poems, and found that the notes to *The Waste

Land were not in it, would demand his money back. But I don't think that these notes did any harm to other poets . . .'

The 'bogus scholarship' Eliot refers to is easily identified by any scholar from his own experience: the lengthy quotation from Ovid, in the original Latin; the passage from Chapman's *Handbook of Birds of Eastern North America*; the reference to a pamphlet on *The Proposed Demolition of Nineteen City Churches* – these and similar references are the devices we all use from time to time to dress up or pad out our own work, and they have led to the notion that Eliot's notes are a parody of scholarship (the apparatus of *The Waste Land* so infuriated William Carlos Williams that he could think of *Paterson* as 'a reply to Greek and Latin with the bare hands'). Many of the notes *are* 'bogus', but only in their lack of proportion. As I shall illustrate in a few moments, every detail in the notes – no matter how trivial – refers to some stage in the imaginative growth of the poem. The problem is not whether to accept or reject the information, but how to weigh and use it. This is exactly the problem Eliot is getting at, obliquely, in 'The Frontiers of Criticism', which might have been subtitled: 'An attempt to establish sensible frontiers for criticism of *The Waste Land*'.

'The Frontiers of Criticism' is a deeply divided essay, divided by the tension between Eliot's critical theory on the one hand (which rejects any attempt to trace the work of art back into its origins, and sees the work as self-sufficient and autonomous), and on the other his own poetic practice and that of his contemporaries (which relies explicitly on the identification of allusions and the recognition of echoes). In the essay Eliot focuses his concern on two works that seem to him to lie beyond the frontiers of normal criticism: one is John Livingston Lowes's famous source study, *The Road to Xanadu*; the other is Joyce's *Finnegans Wake*. *The Road to*

Xanadu fascinated Eliot because, for all its seductive interest (really the interest one has in a piece of detection), it dramatizes a radical and irreducible gap between the writer's sources and his finished creation. Lowes, like Coleridge, was an omnivorous reader, and in *The Road to Xanadu* he traces to their originals the countless 'borrowed images or phrases' that make up the texture of *Kubla Khan* and *The Ancient Mariner*. But in spite of the vast amount of fascinating material thrown up by Lowes's research, the book has almost no 'critical' value. As Eliot comments, 'No one, after reading this book, could suppose that he understood *The Ancient Mariner* any better.' Nor does the book add much to our knowledge of the creative imagination: when faced with the actual process by which Coleridge's reading was transformed into art, all Lowes can do is quote Ariel's song from *The Tempest*, mutter something about a sea-change, and pass by. Eliot himself can do no better, since – when discussing Coleridge in *The Use of Poetry and the Use of Criticism* – he remarks that the imagery of *Kubla Khan*, 'whatever its origins in Coleridge's reading, sank to the depths of Coleridge's feeling, was saturated, transformed there – "those are pearls that were his eyes" – and brought up into daylight again.'

So *The Road to Xanadu*, as Eliot reads it, would seem to place a bar before most source-hunting and genetic criticism, warning us away from the manuscript evidence and the direction pointed out by the notes to *The Waste Land*. And yet there is the troubling presence of *Finnegans Wake*, that pyrrhic victory of the major tendencies in modernist art, where the process of composition is part of the book's subject-matter, and where the sources are an indispensable – one might almost say the sole – route to the work's structure and meaning. It is no accident that the best critical studies of *Finnegans Wake*, Clive Hart's *Structure and Motif in 'Finne-*

gans Wake' and J. S. Atherton's *The Books at the Wake*, are source-studies reminiscent of Lowes.

So here is the puzzle of a critical theory that resists any attempt to explain poetry 'in terms of something else,' coupled with a poetic technique that constantly drives our attention toward other works or toward the poet's private experience. Eliot confesses in the same essay that his own best criticism consists of 'essays on poets and poetic dramatists who had influenced me', and is 'a by-product of my private poetry-workshop; or a prolongation of the thinking that went into the formation of my own verse'. Yet he would not wish us to read his poetry through his criticism. The theoretical problem thus stated, like all important problems in literary criticism, would appear to be insoluble on the level of theory. But in practice it is of course a problem that can be effectively handled, at least in pragmatic fashion, by readers of good sense and judgment. I am reminded of Eliot's famous statement in *After Strange Gods* that 'in one's prose reflexions one may be legitimately occupied with ideals, whereas in the writing of verse [and, I might add, in practical criticism] one can only deal with actuality'.

The actuality of *The Waste Land*'s relation to its sources is partially revealed through what we know of the process of composition. The poem was largely written at Margate and Lausanne during the last three months of 1921, while Eliot was recuperating from a spiritual and physical breakdown. In a very real sense the writing of the poem was an act of reintegration, both of Eliot's personality and of his ten-year journey through the vortex of literary experiment. In retrospect, every aspect of his personal or literary experience available to us from the years 1920–1922 seems to point directly toward *The Waste Land*. For example, during 1921 and 1922 Eliot wrote a series of London letters for both the American and French audiences, published in *The*

Dial and *Nouvelle Revue Française*: enter this material at any point and we are immediately confronted with another note to *The Waste Land*. In the London Letter to *The Dial* dated May 1921 Eliot closes with a gloomy note on the potential destruction of several Wren churches in the City of London, churches whose great beauty redeems 'some vulgar street' or the 'hideous banks and commercial houses'. He contrasts by implication the frenzied business houses with the near-empty churches, 'fallen into desuetude', and he concludes in this fashion:

'To one who, like the present writer, passes his days in this City of London (*quand'io sentii chiavar l'uscio di sotto*) the loss of these towers, to meet the eye down a grimy lane, and of these empty naves, to receive the solitary visitor at noon from the dust and tumult of Lombard Street, will be irreparable and unforgotten. A small pamphlet issued for the London County Council (Proposed Demolition of Nineteen City Churches: P. S. King & Son, Ltd., 2–4 Gt. Smith Street, Westminster, S. W. 1, 3s. 6d. net) should be enough to persuade of what I have said.'

This passage leads directly into two of the most moving and important sections of *The Waste Land*. The parenthetical reference to *Inferno* xxxiii shows that Eliot associated his own 'imprisonment' in the City of London with Ugolino's imprisonment in the horrible tower. Ugolino, imprisoned and doomed to starve to death, heard the key turn below in the tower; the speaker at the end of *The Waste Land*, after reciting the ritual command to 'sympathize', confesses:

> I have heard the key
> Turn in the door once and turn once only
> We think of the key, each in his prison
> Thinking of the key, each confirms a prison

In the note to this passage Eliot refers us to Canto XXXIII of the *Inferno*, quotes the same phrase used in the London Letter, and then connects it with one of F. H. Bradley's remarks on the sealed-off nature of personal experience.

The other half of the passage from the London Letter leads directly to the vision of the City of London which occurs midway through *The Waste Land*:

> 'This music crept by me upon the waters'
> And along the Strand, up Queen Victoria Street.
> O City city, I can sometimes hear
> Beside a public bar in Lower Thames Street,
> The pleasant whining of a mandoline
> And a clatter and a chatter from within
> Where fishmen lounge at noon: where the walls
> Of Magnus Martyr hold
> Inexplicable splendour of Ionian white and gold.

Magnus Martyr, by the foot of London Bridge, was one of the Wren churches slated for destruction, and Eliot duly refers us in the notes to the pamphlet on *The Proposed Demolition of Nineteen City Churches*.

A similar pastiche of *données* for the poem can be found in the first paragraph of the London Letter for July 1921. London has been basking under a 'hot rainless spring', Eliot tells his American audience; 'a new form of influenza has been discovered, which leaves extreme dryness and a bitter taste in the mouth'; but paradoxically, the 'blazing glare' has revealed for 'the first time towers and steeples of an uncontaminated white'. But in spite of the promise of the white towers, the dry spring has been accompanied by a cultural drought – the opera has deserted London, and Eliot compares himself by allusion to a victim of the Babylonian captivity: 'They have forgotten thee, O Sion.' In one way or another, all of these details later enter into the atmosphere and texture of *The Waste Land*, and the obscure allusion to Psalm 137 finds its counterpart at the beginning of Part III of the poem, where the speaker interjects a personal confession – 'By the waters of Leman I sat down and wept.'

All these details I have been recounting would seem to be perfect raw materials for some successor to John Livingston Lowes, interested in how the poem grew out of Eliot's reading and experience (perhaps the book will be called *The Road to Margate Sands*). But for the literary critic these details are at best peripheral, and at worst distracting; they belong to Eliot's biography, or to some investigation of the creative process, not to literary criticism as a study of form and context. They lie on the other side of the frontier Eliot was trying to establish in his 1956 lecture, and they make his fretful handling of the notes a good deal clearer. In effect, Eliot padded out the fundamental notes (the identifications of quotations and obvious allusions) with material from the private genesis of the poem, and therefore he well knew that he had invited – and even sanctioned – the investigation of another John Livingston Lowes.

But if Eliot's writings and reading of 1920 and 1921 are littered with the unassimilated raw materials of *The Waste Land*, which are not our immediate business, they also reveal 'sources' or influences of a quite different kind, and these are very much the business of responsible criticism. Certain names run like *leitmotifs* through Eliot's writing and reading during the gestation period of *The Waste Land*, and they suggest the major forces which shaped his imagination at that time, and which – since they were shared in large measure by Ezra Pound – also shaped the joint process that turned a sequence of related poems into the highly articulated poem we now know. These names are F. H. Bradley, Henry James, Joseph Conrad, Pound himself, Sir James Frazer, and James Joyce. In conclusion, I would like to comment briefly on some of these writers, since it seems to me that Eliot's responses to them offer the best chances for new perspectives on *The Waste Land* itself.

It is no accident that all but one of these writers worked in prose, and that the one poet – Ezra Pound – had impressed upon Eliot his famous motto, 'Poetry should be at least as well written as prose'; by which Pound meant that most contemporary verse could not match the intensity and concentration found in the best fiction of Flaubert or Joyce. In a manner of speaking, *The Waste Land* brought to poetry many of the special achievements of the modern novel, both in its manipulation of narrative perspective and in its density of presentation. Although Eliot obviously did not feel that 'the "long poem" is a thing of the past', he did believe that 'there must be more in it it for the length than our grandparents seemed to demand; and for us, anything that can be said as well in prose can be said better in prose'. Later, after his work on the *Quartets*, Eliot came to believe that the 'long poem' needed a formula of alternating concentration and expansion, with passages of low intensity to set off the *symboliste* moments, but at the time of *The Waste Land* he clearly had in mind an ideal for the 'long poem' not far from that of Edgar Allan Poe: an extended work of sustained lyrical intensity that could be absorbed at one sitting, or – to put it in spatial terms – an extended work that could still be grasped by the mind as a single Image, an emotional and intellectual complex apprehended in an instant of time (to paraphrase the Imagist manifesto). It is this ideal of compression that governed all of Pound's suggestions for revision, and that lies behind his final compliment: 'The thing now runs from "April . . ." to "shantih" without a break. That is

19 pages, and let us say the longest poem in the English langwidge. Don't try to bust all records by prolonging it three pages further.' In effect, the tightening up of *The Waste Land* was like Joyce's collapsing of *Stephen Hero* into the 'spots of time' that are *A Portrait of the Artist*: the aim was a work of art which, in Conrad's motto, would carry its justification for existence in every line.

In his 'Preface to Modern Literature', first published in May 1922, Eliot bracketed Joyce and Conrad as twin masters of those modern fictional techniques, initially explored by Henry James, which are 'struggling to digest and express new objects, new groups of objects, new feelings, new aspects' (he had made the same association earlier in his Swinburne essay). Among the techniques Eliot had in mind was clearly the manipulation of point-of-view, a hallmark of recent experimental fiction. The central *persona* of *The Waste Land* owes more to James's 'central consciousness' and Conrad's detached narrator than to the various *personae* found in the poetry of Yeats and Pound. The method that makes Tiresias, 'although a mere spectator and not indeed a "character",' the 'most important personage in the poem, uniting all the rest', is a method Eliot learned by going to school to modern fiction. He once thought of using a citation from Conrad's 'Heart of Darkness' ('The horror! the horror!') as an epigraph for the poem, but the debt to Conrad's narrative method is much more pervasive than any particular connection with the desperate vision of Mr. Kurtz.

Two other pairings from Eliot's prose of this time strike me as significant. One is the similarity in his discussions of Joyce and Frazer; the other is his constant association of Henry James with F. H. Bradley. At the time when *The Waste Land* was written Frazer had just finished condensing the twelve volumes of *The Golden Bough* into one, and

Eliot took this as an occasion to define the 'profound influence' Frazer's anthropology had exercised upon his generation. In one essay he discussed Frazer under the startling rubric 'A Vitalizing of the Classics', which might seem more appropriate to Joyce's *Ulysses*; and in *The Dial*'s London Letter dated September 1921 he discussed *The Golden Bough* in connection with Stravinsky's *Rites of Spring*.

'The effect was like *Ulysses* with illustrations by the best contemporary illustrator . . . The spirit of the music was modern, and the spirit of the ballet was primitive ceremony. The Vegetation Rite upon which the ballet is founded remained, in spite of the music, a pageant of primitive culture. It was interesting to any one who had read *The Golden* Bough and similar works, but hardly more than interesting. In art there should be interpenetration and metamorphosis. Even *The Golden Bough* can be read in two ways: as a collection of entertaining myths, or as a revelation of that vanished mind of which our mind is a continuation. In everything in the *Sacre du Printemps*, except in the music, one missed the sense of the present. Whether Stravinsky's music be permanent or ephemeral I do not know; but it did seem to transform the rhythm of the steppes into the scream of the motor horn, the rattle of machinery, the grind of wheels, the beating of iron and steel, the roar of the underground railway, and the other barbaric cries of modern life; and to transform these despairing noises into music.'

In short, Eliot found in Frazer and in Joyce the same 'point of view', the same 'vision' – the terms are his – which brought past and present into juxtaposition through myth and ritual. And it is surely this 'vision', rather than any particular use of a mythological narrative, that Eliot had in mind when he wrote '*Ulysses*, Order, and Myth'. It is a vision particularly congenial to the literary ideals of

'Tradition and the Individual Talent', one which suggests that Eliot may have learned a great deal more from Joyce's handling of 'Lycidas' and the death-by-water theme than he did from Joyce's use of the *Odyssey*. This is supported by the fact that the 'Proteus' episode of *Ulysses*, which bears the closest analogies to *The Golden Bough*, passed through Eliot's hands in 1918, while he could not have seen the overall shape of Joyce's dependence on the *Odyssey* until after *The Waste Land* had been partially drafted.

I would like to ring one more change upon two names that echo through Eliot's prose of 1921–1922: F. H. Bradley (the subject of Eliot's doctoral thesis) and Henry James. Once again, as with Joyce and Frazer, it is the essential 'vision' of these two men that Eliot finds compelling. He had long admired James, both as a master of psychological prose and as an example of the successful expatriate who never lost his peculiar qualities as an American writer. Like Pound, Eliot had contributed to the 1918 issue of *The Little Review* dedicated to James, and in his essay 'Prediction in Regard to Three English Authors', first published in 1923, he linked James with Bradley as a 'master of thought' as well as a 'master of art'. Eliot obviously saw in the novelist and the philosopher two congenial minds, each aware of 'the disparity between possibility and fact', and Bradley's famous description of the plight of the individual personality (quoted in the notes to *The Waste Land*) applies equally well to the plight of one of Henry James's 'poor gentlemen': 'My external sensations are no less private to myself than are my thoughts or my feelings. In either case my experience falls within my own circle, a circle closed on the outside; and, with all its elements alike, every sphere is opaque to the others which surround it . . . the whole world for each is peculiar and private to that soul.'

From first to last in Eliot's poetic career, from the undersea vision of Prufrock through the Hyacinth garden of *The Waste Land* to the rose garden of 'Burnt Norton', it is a quintessentially Jamesian experience which lies at the heart of his work. The tragedy is that of one who can perceive but cannot act, who can understand and remember but cannot communicate. 'I could not/Speak, and my eyes failed, I was neither/ Living nor dead . . ./ Looking into the heart of light, the silence.' At one time Eliot thought of titling the second part of *The Waste Land* 'In the Cage', an obvious reference to James's novella where the little telegraph girl, shut into her wire cage, can only live vicariously through the communications that pass across her desk. She knows everything, and can act upon nothing: she is like Tiresias, who knows all, foresuffers all, and can prevent none of it.

This is the vision of personal isolation that Eliot shares with James, and that lies at the deepest reaches of all his works. And yet, like James, Eliot was possessed with the complementary 'vision of an ideal society'; the result was an art aware at every turn of the 'disparity between possibility and fact'. In his later works Eliot does explore ways of breaking the 'closed circle of consciousness', through discipline or through grace. But in *The Waste Land* the only consolation lies in memory and the vicarious ordering of past experience: 'These fragments I have shored against my ruins.' For those who need help in reaching the emotional centre of *The Waste Land*, the surest guide lies not in Miss Jessie Weston's *From Ritual to Romance*, but in Henry James's 'The Beast in the Jungle' and *The Sacred Fount*.

Eliot in His Time, Oxford University Press

Roland Mathias **Lord Cutglass, Twenty Years After**

'It sometimes seems,' wrote John Ackerman in number 49 of *The Anglo-Welsh Review*, 'as though there are two ways of disliking [Dylan] Thomas: one is to dislike him, the other to disparage the later poems.' And that is, I believe, a fairly accurate summing up of the position of such detractors as dare to show their heads in 1973. I shall not, in this article, be concerned directly with the 'disliking', except in so far as this may be seen as arising out of a conflict between the poet and his natural environment – more specifically, as having to do with the degree of his Welshness – and it is no part of my intention to go into the frequent excesses and the chronic wretchedness of the poet's life. My purpose is two-fold: first, to look at certain aspects of Dylan Thomas's childhood and upbringing which appear to determine the degree of his Welshness and, not at all incidentally, his attitude to poetry, and second, to ascertain whether these aspects reflect, in the end, on the later poems – which have, in the last decade, become the King Charles's Head of any critical operation.

Perhaps we are now far enough away in time to treat the facts of Dylan's youth and upbringing with the 'distancing' objectivity which the academic approach expects. And perhaps not. I remember, if still with some astonishment, how taken aback I was when, in attempting to raise a collection for Caitlin, on the news of Dylan's death in New York, I had to deal with a deputation which, with some hostility, urged me to drop the idea. The deputation did not, as it happens, represent what might be called the prim or the Nonconformist element in the community. It did, indeed, object to the 'life' of the poet, but even more to what was felt to be the anti-

Welshness, the general disservice to Wales which Dylan's attitude had appeared to represent. I was surprised then, and readers accustomed to years of an assessment which is, ostensibly, purely literary will be surprised now. But the two responses which Dylan evoked in Wales cannot simply be divided into the suspicion and the hostility of Welsh-speakers on the one hand and the pride and amusement of English-speakers on the other. The original equivocation which provoked them was there in the nature of the poet himself. His own attitude to Wales was based first on deprivation and the clever hostility that sometimes comes from it, then on a gradual realization of loss and a disillusionment with the ambitions that had created that loss (in his parents and himself). My thesis is not merely that these factors reveal themselves in the letters and ultimately, if less clearly, in the poetry, but that the first phase, even after its personal effects had appeared to fade, remained definitive, even limiting, in the poetry – particularly perhaps in the later poems by which many critics assume that Dylan Thomas stands or falls.

Outside Wales people experienced, and experience, some difficulty in understanding the duality of response from readers and hearers which was characteristic of Dylan's reputation in his lifetime, because they tend to believe that his life was typical of that of the uninhibited Celt, that he wrote as he did *because* he was Welsh (in terms of his subject-preoccupations and of the grandness of the manner) and that as a poet he was a Welsh type, that is, he rose naturally from a Welsh background. Some of these assumptions are, if not absolutely wrong, much more dubiously based than is commonly realized. They take their colour from the superficialities of the poet's names – Dylan, the golden-haired boy of the *Mabinogion* story, *Dylan Eil Ton*, Sea Son of the Wave who became at once 'a part of the sea', and Marlais, the bardic name of his nineteenth century great-uncle, who earned a reputation both as a radical preacher and as a poet. These names, which fit his father's attitude to the Welsh heritage so little, can be explained only as a momentary atavism created by the fact of a son's birth. Nothing else about Dylan (a name which he was quite content to have pronounced *Dillen* or *Dillun* by his cronies) was anywhere near as Welsh as this involuntary prefix. Let me explain this view more fully.

In the first place he was born in Swansea, which in the eighteenth century was well-known as an *English* watering-place, a resort of the upper classes and minor literary figures like Walter Savage Landor. Number 5 Cwmdonkin Drive is a house in a very steep street in the Uplands area, which, with Mumbles and Sketty and the places between, best exemplified the Little Englander complex. Dylan Thomas knew almost no Welsh himself and would have heard none amongst his playmates, most of them the sons of shopkeepers or aspiring professional men. When he was a boy, two-thirds of the people of Swansea spoke English only, and scarcely any were monoglot Welsh. Yet north-west of the town, away from the English-speaking playground of Gower, the old, agricultural Wales of 'the good, bad boys from the lonely farms' rubbed shoulders with the Welshness of the miners of Pontardulais and Ammanford, and north-eastwards the Swansea Valley itself, as it climbed only one degree to Morriston and Clydach, echoed with voices more unashamedly Welsh. The real Wales indeed, from its forward points at copper-poisoned Landore, Llangyfelach and Gorseinon, was still watching the privileged, commercial enclave of Swansea, but its representatives were allowed in only to market, to inhabit some of the ramshackle houses in the dock area and to beachcomb in times of holiday. When Dylan Thomas wrote that

> outside, a *strange* Wales, coal-pitted, mountained, river run, full, so far as I knew, of choirs and sheep and story-book tall hats, moved about its business which was none of mine

he was antithesising merrily, writing up what his childhood only part comprehended. But there was an important truth there just the same. He knew *about* Wales right enough; he didn't really imagine the women wore tall hats. But he hadn't been inside the tradition of Wales. He had been to Sunday School when staying with his Aunt 'Dosie' at English-speaking Newton, where his uncle, David Rees, was minister of Paraclete, but this was as a small child. He had no real notion of what it was like, either, morally and spiritually, to have been brought up in the Welsh Nonconformist tradition. What he saw of it he saw from the dissident window of No. 5 Cwmdonkin Drive, from the refuge provided by a lapsed father. Out of that window he was what he calls in 'Do you not father me' *the wanton starer*:

> Sunday in Wales. The Sunday-walkers have slunk out of the warrens in which they sleep and breed all the unholy week, have put on their black suits, reddest eyes, and meanest expressions, and are now marching up the hill past my window . . . I see the rehearsed gestures, the correct smiles, the grey cells revolving around nothing under the godly bowlers. I see the unborn children struggling up the hill in their mothers, beating on the jailing slab of the womb, little realizing what a smugger prison they wish to leap into.

He was writing here to Pamela Hansford Johnson (15 April, 1934) and what he was describing was a rapidly declining sabbatarianism in a Swansea where

Puritan influences had always been weaker than in Welsh-speaking Wales. What we really hear, of course, is the voice of the young satirist identifying himself as made for better things by separating himself from the bourgeois and philistine and provincial environment (*his* probable words, not mine).

Am I not all of you by the directed sea
Where bird and shell are babbling in my tower?
('Do you not father me')

No, indeed not. Most certainly not. Not in that clever adolescence of his.

But the point I have tried to make thus far is the smaller of two. If Dylan Thomas was separated, through no fault of his own, from the older Welshness of Wales, that was a separation shared by hundreds of thousands of others, not a few of them poets and writers. If he added his own personal will to this separation, he was not alone in this either, and the root cause lies in a deprivation that was the more serious because deliberate.

If Swansea was relatively weak in Welsh tradition, it was a lack that his home could have satisfied. But although his parents both spoke Welsh (or had at one time spoken Welsh) they never used the language at No. 5 Cwmdonkin Drive '(the young Dylan's *Glamorgan villa*) with its neo-Georgian respectability, its middle-class decorative gestures in knitted texts and reproduction Greek Statues, and its resident maid' (Walford Davies, *Dylan Thomas*, p. 4). Dylan's father, David John Thomas, who was intellectually and personally the dominant partner, had forsworn his Welshness in a way unfortunately characteristic of many ambitious Welshmen sixty years ago. This particular brand of Dic-Shon-Dafyddism is uncommon now amongst the professional classes of Wales, who may find it hard to appreciate that ethic which insisted that to *get on in the world*, socially, professionally or commercially, it was essential to discard Welsh and embrace English. In the case of David John Thomas the discarding was determined and comprehensive: he had his son and daughter given elocution lessons, at which there was born Lord Cutglass: he cut himself off absolutely from his Welsh-speaking relatives to the west – never going to see them and never letting his children deputise for him: and he had long since severed all connection with the Unitarian practice and tradition of his great-uncle Gwilym Marles, from whose radicalism he had distanced himself even further. The son of a railwayman from Carmarthen, David John Thomas had taken first-class honours in English at the University College of Wales, Aberystwyth: he was a poet manqué, with a fine reading voice but no sufficient poems: he was a good, though severe, teacher with the sort of histrionic talent that possession of such a voice would suggest: and he regarded his position as Senior English Master at Swansea Grammar School as status less than worthy of his academic record. (It may be mentioned, in parenthesis, that he was perhaps not quite unjustified in that opinion. When, in 1922, the post of Professor of English at the new University College was advertised, he applied for it but was passed over. The man ultimately appointed had academic qualifications inferior to his). His library was the library of a particularly alert and well-read teacher of English who was alive to contemporary developments in poetry and drama, but his attitude to life was negative. Indeed, he had chosen literature instead of life, having decided long since to maltreat and sever the lifeline that came down to him.

For the young Dylan, then, this deprivation was decisive. That his mother was still in contact with her relations in Welsh-speaking Wales and sent her son on visits to them was ultimately important but not immediately so, because Dylan, in his cleverly superior adolescence, despised his mother's garrulity and lack of intellect, taking his father's stance in this as in most matters. His Aunt Annie at Llangain and her family, kind as they were to the superior young man who sometimes came and stayed, partook in his mind of his mother's folly and chattering concern. Welsh-speaking Wales, as we shall see, was full of similar mindless dolts.

What was left of the Welsh umbilical cord, what few frayings remained? First, there was the Bible, which D. J. Thomas, though an agnostic, read regularly to his son from his earliest years – the Bible as literature and with it the sonority of D. J.'s voice. That this was of the utmost importance I hope to show later. Of tradition little remained beyond a few oft-told tales of great-great-uncle Gwilym Marles: as a cub reporter on *The Swansea Evening Post* and as young-man-about-the-pubs he heard plenty of gossip about the 'primitives' higher up the Valley and was regaled in The Mermaid at Newton or elsewhere upon his friend Wynford Vaughan Thomas's epics of his mythical preacher Jones Goppa. But friends from a more genuinely Welsh background like Wynford were a rarity: Dylan's Wales was what Swansea knew of it, and the most 'emancipated' part of Swansea at that. In brief, he never had first-hand knowledge of what it felt like to belong to a *Welsh* community – in this respect he was totally unlike, say, Glyn Jones or Idris Davies and perhaps Alun Lewis, wholly or partially bereft of the Welsh language as they too were. He had more in common with Vernon Watkins, who lived first in Swansea and then in Gower and was sent away to school at Repton, but with Vernon the deprivation was circumstantial and gradual, involving none of the initial contempt and the ultimate need for redress that Dylan felt. In the case of Alun Lewis, although he too was sent to boarding school, his roots in the basic radicalism and democratic feeling of Welsh community life were so strong that his poetic sensitivity was unable, in the end, to withstand the weight of the pity and the alienation he felt in India. He died, it may be said, for reasons precisely the opposite of those which hampered Dylan Thomas who, so far from being a product of a Welsh community, had much more in common with boys of the sixties and seventies in not being a product of a community at all. When Dylan made a political or social gesture it was almost always at second-hand. The only letter he ever wrote to the press, dated January 14, 1934, was intended to attack the restrictive attitudes of Non-conformity. In this he urged the editor to give his readers

> some little consciousness of the immoral restrictions placed upon them, of the humbug and smug respectability that works behind them all their handcuffed days, and to do this, not from any political bias, but from the undeniable conviction that the God is not the lukewarm soup and starch of the chapels, but the red hot grains of love and life distributed equally and impartially among us all.

He had been listening, of course, to his left wing Socialist friend Bert Trick (whom he called, wrongly, his 'Communist grocer' and who gave him a severe dressing-down for breaking into print in this way). His own freedom from community pressures of any kind will appear presently and one may well wonder in whom, in the end, the greater smugness lay. His inability to write politically-motivated or socially conscious poems is well-known (the only serious attempt he made here emerged as the virtually abstract 'The hand that signed the paper'), though it must be admitted that there is more to this than a self-centred, romantic attitude and plain ignorance about the nature of the public good.

It may be well at this point to document a little Dylan's early hatred of the Wales which circumscribed Swansea. It was a country of 'miles of desolate fields and scattered farmhouses', in which it was impossible to speak to anyone except about 'the prospect of rain and the quickest way to snare rabbits' (Letter to Pamela Hansford Johnson, late October 1933). At Llangain (his Uncle Tom's house) he could hear 'the beastly little brook that goes gingle-gingle past this room' and had to converse, if only for a few moments, with a man with close-set eyes like those of 'the terrible thing he held in his hand', Billy Fach the ferret. One night 'the long road to Llanstephan (which he had to walk from his Aunt Ann's farm because he was out of cigarettes) was 'bounded by trees and farmers' boys pressed amorously upon the udders of their dairymaids', and in the end there was no cigarette machine in Llanstephan (ditto, early November 1933). It was a crude world of 'farmers . . . sitting at their fires, looking into the blazing wood and thinking of God knows what littlenesses', of stuffed foxes and china dogs, stale ferns, Fauntleroy photographs of himself, insanitary buildings and stupid relatives who spoiled and petted him beyond endurance. On the way to this perpetually rained-upon backwater he had passed through little mining townships where he had seen 'little colliers, diseased in mind and body as only the Welsh can be, standing in groups outside the Welfare Hall'. It was a horrible world, that Wales, and even in London some years later he did not wish to consort with Welshmen unless they had been friends of his in Swansea. To Pamela Hansford Johnson, the penfriend with whom he was already prepared to be in love, he wrote in October 1933:

> It's impossible for me to tell you how much I want to get out of it all, out of the narrowness and dirtiness, out of the eternal ugliness of the

Welsh people and all that belongs to them, out of the pettiness of a mother I don't care for and the giggling batch of relatives . . . I shall have to get out soon or there will be no need. I'm sick and this bloody country's killing me.

As he said on a later occasion,

Land of my fathers, my fathers can keep it.

Much of this self-conscious arrogance soon disappeared. It was, in any case, part of the *âme damnée* pose which he dropped when he found that it did not impress Pamela. But it had another root in his great desire to get to London. 'The fact that I am unemployed helps . . . to add to my natural hatred of Wales' he wrote in March 1934 to Stephen Spender, one of the well-known poets who had already picked out his work as startlingly different. But that unemployment had been deliberately willed, and the mere fact that, irrespective of economics, he saw his *métier* as being in London tells us something important about what his notion of being a poet was.

Perhaps I ought to make plain at this point why I emphasise Dylan's background so strongly. It is because I see in it the key to his poetic development or, rather, the keys, because there was a closing and an opening, not of the same door. Let me indicate first how closely Swansea and the major part of his poetic output are intertwined. Between the ages of fifteen and a half and nineteen and a half Dylan Thomas wrote over 250 poems which he considered successful enough to be transcribed into his four cheap red notebooks (threepenny ones with Danger Don'ts on the back cover) and of these fifty-four, most of them considerably revised, he published in his lifetime. That means that more than half of all the poems he chose to publish (as distinct from those that have been published since by Daniel Jones) were given their basic or original form before he left Swansea. That basic form is, of course, more important in terms of the subject-matter, the poetic preoccupation, it contained, than in its precise connection with the more polished version that appeared in *18 Poems*, *25 Poems* or any later book. It is not my purpose here to examine this subject-matter closely: it must be sufficient to say that whether, using John Donne and others, he attempted a metaphysic of the bodily functions, whether his work was a genuine reflection of a loss of identity in the womb (as David Holbrook would seem to be suggesting in *The Code of Night*) or whether, as Raymond L. Hogler has recently indicated (in *The Anglo-Welsh Review* Nos. 47 & 48), he deliberately played the poetry market until he found a subject-matter and a mode that would make his mark for him in the shortest possible time, one thing is obvious enough: his poetry was inchoate, suffocatingly romantic and obscure, reflecting very little of what might be called objective life and background experience in the community to which he nominally belonged. His revisions, of course, often tend towards clarification and in one or two notable instances they alter the whole tone of what little he had written about that objective life and experience.

His friend Vernon Watkins gave it as his opinion that Dylan had at the age of twenty-four what might be called a religious experience. But then Vernon, who thought the best of everyone, was convinced that Dylan afterwards became 'a Blakean Christian'. This postulated experience affected Dylan's prose immediately and his poetry more slowly, precisely because here he was not writing afresh but revising and modifying older material. The change, Vernon asserted, is most succinctly expressed in 'Once it was the colour of saying', where two pairs of lines indicate the turning point:

The gentle seaslides of saying I must undo
That all the charmingly drowned arise to
  cockcrow and kill.

Now my saying shall be my undoing,
And every stone I wind off like a reel.

Thereafter the *Roget's Thesaurus* formula-writing came to an end and alterations made in the drafts of poems were 'all away from ironical statement and in the direction of religious truth.'

Whether we accept this diagnosis or whether we prefer to talk about the process of growing up and unwinding, about the disillusion with the metropolis that had once gleamed golden like the towers of Samarkand, or about the natural revival of feeling for Wales which almost every Welshman experiences when he's away from it and can see it in balance against other societies and other values, in 1938 (when Dylan was twenty-four) we have a notable example of re-writing which gave us one of his best-known poems. Let us go back to the original version.

In January 1933 Dylan wrote to his friend Trevor Hughes saying that his Aunt Ann was in Carmarthen Infirmary dying of cancer of the womb. Her prospective death lent 'a little welcome melodrama to the drawing-room tragi-comedy of my most uneventful life.' He analysed at length his total unmovedness at the expected disappearance of one who loved him. 'Many summer weeks I spent happily with the cancered aunt on her insanitary farm. She loved me quite inordinately, gave me sweets and money, though she could little afford it, petted, and spoiled me. She writes – is it, I wonder, a past tense yet – regularly. Her postscripts are endearing. She still loves – or loved – me, though I don't know why.' It was, for him, a theatrical occasion upon which he could analyse his own selfishness. On the day of the funeral he wrote a poem into his red notebook which

Professor Ralph Maud's book, *Poet in the Making*, makes available for us. This is the final stanza of that poem;

> Another gossips' toy has lost its use,
> Broken lies buried amid broken toys,
> Of flesh and bone lies hungry for the flies,
> Waits for the natron and the mummy paint
> With dead lips pursed and dry bright eyes,
> Another well of rumours and cold lies
> Has dried and one more joke has lost its point.

Even for 'the cancered aunt on her insanitary farm' this was a ruthlessly cold conclusion.

But in 1938, when he re-wrote it into that well-known poem, 'After the Funeral', he became not merely 'Ann's bard on a raised hearth' but 'a desolate boy who slits his throat/In the dark of the coffin'. The first line, with its satiric intention, remains—

> After the funeral, mule praises, brays,

but the conclusion has become a triumphant paean of remembrance:

> Her flesh was meek as milk, but this skyward
> statue
> With the wild breast and blessed and giant skull
> Is carved from her in a room with a wet window
> In a fiercely mourning house in a crooked year.
> I know her scrubbed and sour humble hands
> Lie with religion in their cramp, her threadbare
> Whisper in a damp word, her wits drilled hollow,
> Her fist of a face died clenched on a round pain;
> And sculptured Ann is seventy years of stone.
> These cloud-sopped, marble hands, this
> monumental
> Argument of the hewn voice, gesture and psalm,

Storm me forever over her grave until
The stuffed lung of the fox twitch and cry Love
And the strutting fern lay seeds on the black sill.

Here the old disenchantment is exorcised by the deliberate use of those cold front-parlour ornaments, the stuffed fox and the stale fern: their 'activity' activates all that was previously trivial and stagnant and stale-smelling: the poem is not merely the vindication of that Welsh rural atmosphere which the stories were to complete – it accepts the validity of the religious convention that was central to that atmosphere, the *scrubbed and sour humble hands*, the fierceness of the mourning, the idea that somehow this mourning can and will ultimately be contained in the graveyard statue, so that the *scrubbed and sour humble hands* become *cloud-sopped, marble* and are fixed forever in a speaking gesture which points heavenward, is psalmic. This *monumental argument*, the poet is telling us, *storms* him *forever* now.

It is a complete reversal of the arrogance of those letters to Pamela, but it uses the same vision, turning it inside out. It's not a new, matured vision which has a different slant, which is mediated through developing and thoughtful ideas based on other experience. This is partly because it is *remembered – re-remembered*, if you like – but it is basic to my argument that this new, developing thought is missing from Dylan Thomas's later work in any case. Indeed, another look is needed here at his childhood and youth if we are to reach a conclusion both about the degree of his *Anglo-Welshness* and about the relation of that childhood and youth to the nature and quality of the later poems.

Spoiling of children in a Welsh community used to be the rule rather than the exception (though I hasten to comment that that spoiling had nothing in common with the modern 'buying' or bribing of the child by the provision of *things* – toys, machines and so on – as a substitute for personal attention). But such spoiling almost always stopped short of going soft on academic effort. The Welsh boy had to work hard at school and college. Education was deemed by almost everybody of the first importance. But Dylan's mother was so soft with him that a sickly child with weak lungs and what his wife Caitlin afterwards called 'those chicken bones of his' was allowed to stay away from school altogether until he was seven and to retire to bed whenever life became too much for him (which was frequently). In the result he did exactly what he wanted, misbehaving badly outside and retiring to the safe haven of home whenever the going got rough. Undoubtedly the personal incompetence and indiscipline of his later life begin here: the self-centredness too. He wrote poems, tens and hundreds of them, from the beginning, but he would do nothing else, not even when he went to Swansea Grammar School. He was top in English and bottom in every other subject and not even his father's presence as a member of staff could prevent it. Moreover, having long ago routed his mother, he resisted his father's wish that he should go to university by a cunning insistence that he wanted nothing except to be a poet – a ploy which he knew, or guessed, touched his father's deepest ambition for him. These facts are important only in so far as they reveal, first, that the concept of duty, however lightly phrased, and wherever directed – to his parents, his school or the community of which he was ostensibly part – had never had great meaning for him and that *involvement* (except in an exercise like the school magazine which was closely related to his real apprenticeship) was almost entirely absent from his experience: second, that his education, except in English literature, was remarkably limited and his sense of any wider academic discipline small: and third, that his conception of being a poet was single-minded, professional, individualistic, exclusive of all else. The second and third factors impelled me to state elsewhere that Dylan Thomas was not so much an Anglo-Welsh poet as a poet *à l'anglaise*, and although I can now see factors possibly no less weighty which would point to the opposite conclusion the matter is so essentially arguable that it is worth examining it in more detail.

It was in his father's brown study (those words are to be taken literally) that he read voluminously and 'wrote imitations of whatever I happened, moon-and-print struck, to be goggling at and gorging at the time'. His father read Shakespeare to him at the age of four, sweeping his mother's protests aside. The same resonant voice read the Bible to him frequently. In later recollection he wrote:

> I bulldozed through print, tore through the babbling dead like a tank with a memory. On the very green fields of my youth I stomped pun-shod and neigh-nonnied in a nosebag of adjectives. I *had* to imitate and parody, consciously and unconsciously: I had to try to learn what made words tick, beat, blaze, because I wanted to write what I wanted to write before I knew how to write or what I wanted to.

He is admitting there to the precedence both of the desire to write and the preoccupation with words over the emergence of a subject-matter which of itself might compel him to write. But certainly the breadth of his preparatory reading was all but incredible for one of his age. What we need to understand clearly is that this reading was done, all of it, so that the poet might learn his trade, vocationally, not for any high and general academic ideal. Indeed, the whole academic approach became more and more hateful to Dylan because, in the first place, he had chosen to ignore it, because, in the second place and consequentially, he had failed academically, and because, in the third place and again consequentially, he began to develop an inferiority complex about it. His deficiencies began to show in his twenties: he was still sharp, he picked up a lot at second-hand – but the young man who had commented so precociously on Pamela Hansford-Johnson's poems, whose knowledge of the 'scene' made his reviews of published poetry so masterly, whose perceptions of the literariness of some of Vernon Watkins's cadences were near-infallible, the young man, in brief, who had so spectacularly chosen literature instead of life, never really added much to his poetic material, after he left Swansea, from the reservoir of an educated and thoughtful mind. That he could write brilliant film-scripts is not in doubt: technically he remained second to none. But his reading fell away and he had never, since he went into the cloud of his poetry-packed adolescence, been either a thinker or more than an intensely subjective observer of a wider life. It was this lack of development, I believe, that made him so often refuse to answer questions on the occasion of his many readings and recitals. He would read in that organ voice of his and refuse to speak thereafter. He was sure that the academics were getting at him or would want to get at him and he was equally sure that if he began to argue he would be found out. It is not surprising that he retreated, for his subject-matter, into the one region where criticism could not follow him, the one region where subjective memory had a validity equal to or even superior to that of fact – the world of childhood. Old insanitary Fern Hill became the perfect refuge.

That extraordinary early fertility, I suspect, had exhausted itself. Once it was all words, 'Once it was the colour of saying', and when he began to feel that a development of thought from the original crux was required, he found it increasingly difficult to provide. Was he played out as a poet? Was his legend incommoded by his living as long as he did? What kind of a poet did he consider himself to be?

Early in November 1933 he referred in a letter to Pamela Hansford Johnson to a 'damned diabetic doctor' who had told him he had only four years to live. This statement he made several times, always to people who did not know him well or were not in a position to check his health. All his life he had been dying every time he took a knock and undoubtedly the image of the damned, doomed and dissolute poet he was creating required the suggestion that he had TB. Rayner Heppenstall recalled that in February 1936 he and Dylan went to a pub in the morning.

> As we went out into the cold Dylan began to cough and spit.
> He looked down at his spittle in the roadway and said: 'Blood, boy! That's the stuff.'

There was nothing seriously wrong with his lungs. Had he not indeed won the cross-country at school several times? But the image he required was one of early death. His father had cancer of the tongue in 1933: Dylan was already, as Professor Maud has noted, 'a veteran graveyard poet'. But in whose image was he making himself? I haven't the smallest doubt. It was that of John Keats. The name of Keats comes up in his letters more often, far more often, than that of any other poet. *He* was a lyric poet and he died at the age of twenty-six of tuberculosis. Very significantly, at the end of his life Dylan said to John Davenport: 'I can't go on. I've already had twice as much of it as Keats had.' If it was turning out to be a distance-race after all, he had employed the wrong tactics at the beginning.

These points, then, are all connected. Dylan wasn't going to educate himself in full because there wasn't time. As Constantine Fitzgibbon remarked of him, 'A man who is to be hanged next week will not start to learn Chinese . . . All his life the clocks ticked away his death for him as they did for his Lord Cutglass in *Under Milk Wood.*' Lord Cutglass, you will remember, was his nickname amongst friends in Swansea. It was quite plain *whose* metaphorical house was full of clocks.

This needs to be related ultimately to what I said earlier about possible effects upon his later work. But for the moment I am concerned to 'place' Dylan, to set him in his true relationship with Wales and the poets whom we call Anglo-Welsh. Was he recognisably a Welshman in his poetry? When Fitzgibbon said that 'no major English poet has ever been as Welsh as was Dylan' he was begging too many questions for his statement to have any value. Let me assemble first those points which suggest that he saw himself as an *English* poet who happened, by accident of birth, to belong to the geographical area of Wales.

Amongst these I do not, of course, count his use of the English language and the priority he gave to that. Any Anglo-Welsh poet, compelled by his linguistic inheritance, must necessarily do the same. But we have seen – and this is the true first point – that his literary field of reference was entirely English, by his father's decision. He was deliberately cut off from such Welsh traditions and influences as might reasonably have affected the subject-matter of his writing. This point is underlined by his own endorsement of his father's attitude, by his self-regard, by his non-involvement in a Welshness of life which was available, if in diluted form, even in Swansea. Secondly, this Englishness of his field of reference is given active form in his desire to go to London. This was where, he believed, English poetry was born and made. Thirdly, his intent to be a poet and nothing else was intensely romantic and integral to the English romantic tradition. Poets in Welsh were almost always part of the community, writing for it: they were part-time poets, farmers, shopkeepers, shepherds, preachers, teachers: they did not see themselves primarily as individualists and romantics because they had another position from which to see the community and contribute to it. Anglo-Welsh poets of the first generation tended to inherit this attitude. Dylan, in insisting that he was never to be anything other than a poet, was accepting an alien model. Although he was for a time a reporter, he equivocated even about this brief experience in his first letter to Glyn Jones when he said: 'I am not unemployed for the reason that I have never been employed.' It was an untruth fashioned for his image.

Fourthly, his precocity, inseparable in practice from his notion of the full-time romantic poet who had not long to live, was no part of Welsh practice. It was generally believed in Wales that the poet spoke to his fellows from *experience*, and it was therefore advisable to be old enough to have some. Fifthly and sixthly, his dismissal of education, so dear to the Welsh heart, and the absence in him of any noticeable social commitment – again alien to the socialism or radicalism of genuinely Welsh communities – all mark him as non-Welsh, like his accent. It was certainly an oddity that England in the thirties produced, in Auden, Spender, Day Lewis and MacNeice, a dominant group of poets whose philosophy of poetry was in these last respects close to the Welsh practice, while Wales sent to London a sonorous romantic for whom the matter of society seemed to have little interest.

The fact remains, however, that Dylan was recognized as a Welshman by more than the 'instant Dylan' he could turn on for his cronies. The Welshness was there, it was asserted, in the poetry. What does this mean?

The first answer I would give is perhaps superficial when it is isolated, but as part of a complex of answers it is true enough. Many readers recognized a biblical tone about much of his work, partly a matter of vocabulary – an Authorized Version atmosphere, generated by words that are short, basic and old-fashioned rather than fashionable. Here is the first stanza of 'Before I knocked', one of the best of his earlier poems:

> Before I knocked and flesh let enter,
> With liquid hands tapped on the womb,
> I who was shapeless as the water
> That shaped the Jordan near my home
> Was brother to Mnetha's daughter
> And sister to the fathering worm.

Even more the last two lines of a later stanza:

> My heart knew love, my belly hunger;
> I smelt the maggot in my stool.

The Old Testament is perhaps the most obvious provider, but we cannot ignore Donne (the *Devotions* as well as the *Poems*), Blake, whose *Prophetic Books* gave Dylan the obscure Mnetha he mentions, and Milton. The Welsh, of course, have no exclusive rights to the Bible and the effect of the vocabulary on its own is, as Dylan's reading would suggest it ought to be, Anglo-Saxon. It is the language shaped during and after Elizabethan times by the Puritan tradition – even if that language is used for strange and seemingly unPuritanical purposes.

Why do I suggest, then, that a Biblical tone is a Welsh quality? Well, the word *tone* is the key. It is tone, not vocabulary, that suggests Welshness in Dylan. And the tone is a preaching tone, a sonorous-ness of delivery, very occasionally rising to *hwyl*, but never falling to the conversational. It has been suggested that this tone is a manifestation of *bardic impersonality*, but I see little contact with the bardic in Dylan's story. Instead I hear the cadences of the voice of David John Thomas as he read the Bible to his young son, the cadences of a man who thought he had cut off his Welsh heritage for good but nevertheless carried ineradicably in his voice-habit the remembrance of the old Welsh preachers of West Wales. The Bible was literature, the language often poetry. Could the young Dylan have failed to associate his father's tone with it? Doubtless Wynford Vaughan Thomas on many occasions subsequently simulated the *hwyl* of the Rev. Jones Goppa. Wales was full of action stories of preachers in those days.

Then, closely associated with it – and another function of the preaching zeal which was part of Dylan's being without his knowing it – was the habit of *affirmation*. Very often one may feel that the affirmation is based on nothing or next to nothing – what can be offered, for instance, as a logical lead-up to the repeated declaration that 'Death shall have no dominion'? Undoubtedly the reader, especially when reading or listening to the early poems, assumes that he is dealing with a profound and complicated metaphysic and that the affirmation appears to him isolated only because he has not understood what went before. But as the poems became more 'open', this affirmatory style, enormously successful as it is, can be seen to be standing up on its own. If we take the 'argument' of 'A Refusal to Mourn the Death, by Fire, of a Child in London' (to my mind one of the most enduringly attractive of all Dylan's poems) we may ask, cynically, what kind of *other* death the reader was foolishly expecting. And what kind of assurance is it that prompts the poet so dramatically to refuse to mourn? Is it sufficient, as the poem does, to suggest that the child goes to join the 'first dead' and becomes one with the Earth-Mother in corruption and – corruption and what? Rebirth? Is it because the child's body enters the vegetable cycle that it will never afterwards suffer death? It is not my purpose here to pursue the meaning of this poem or others. I merely want to suggest that the strength of the affirmation is disproportionate to the strength of the supposed reasons for it. This, again, is an aspect of the preacher's manner – and I intend no cynicism: in a brief sermon there usually isn't time for all the run-up arguments, only for the asseverative conclusion.

Is this Welsh? No, not specifically. Zeal is a characteristic of poor and unprivileged societies everywhere. But Dylan was in Wales and of Wales and there can be no question where he got it from.

Perhaps I may touch on another point which emerges from the same poem. It *sounds* intensely religious. No, that is inexact, there are present in it religious or sacramental terms which seem integral to its argument: *the round/Zion of the water bead, the synagogue of the ear of corn, salt seed, valley of sackcloth, stations of the breath.* All this is there to strengthen and validate the affirmation, though the affirmation itself is not Christian at all. It would not be difficult to point to instances of the use of Christian terminology which are blasphemous – 'my Jack of Christ' will serve for one – and one is compelled to the conclusion that this terminology, this particular imagery, *comes in a package with* the affirmation – not perhaps out of deliberate intention to mislead or deceive so much as out of an inability to separate one element of the inheritance from the other. Dylan was unusually dependent on that earliest period of his life for the poetic images he developed. That Biblical terminology was there, part of him, inextricably, even though he often wished to use it for different and, as we should think, strange purposes.

There is the Welshness, then. The Nonconformist preaching tradition with all its outward trappings but deprived of the faith that fired it. The tone of voice not entirely typical, but constant – *part* of poetry for him. He was like a Puritan version of the lapsed priest (see Joyce: *Ulysses*, Pt. II, sect. 12 as a source for *Under Milk Wood*).

I must, however, mention briefly one other consideration. Although Dylan Thomas began by experimenting with free verse the main body of his poetry is characterized by a determination to achieve and impose on the thought the most demanding form. It is, I believe, useless to talk about an inheritance from Welsh poetry, in which the *cynghanedd* and the *awdl* in particular had for centuries appeared to place intricacy of form above poetic content – useless because Dylan could not have read such poems and never displayed (unlike Gerard Manley Hopkins) any interest in them. How, then, do we explain this special passion? Vernon Watkins, saying of himself that he didn't care for tennis without a net, added that Dylan Thomas would have liked two nets. To explain this passion for poetic form as in some way native to a Welshman I feel to be highly dangerous and in the end unsupportable by argument. Nor am I very much happier with the idea that Dylan saw the poet as *maker* – in the sense of craftsman – which was part of the bardic tradition, for the reason that I have already mentioned, that he knew little or nothing of that tradition. We must simply accept two similarities that cannot be adequately connected by argument – the tradition of formal intricacy in Welsh poetry and the kind of demanding versification to which Dylan Thomas felt impelled, a form in which at first he packed his images so tightly that the narrative or thought line was obscured and later the individual line was so decorated verbally that the effect is sometimes as cloying as the earlier works were difficult. Where, one asks oneself helplessly, where in all his reading of Keats, Milton, Donne and others, did he find anything like his plan for the Prologue to the *Collected Poems*, in which 102 lines rhyme 1 with 102, 2 with 101 and so on? One can see the derivation of the 'Vision and Prayer' poems, shaped on the page, from George Herbert, whom we know he had read and studied. But what of the others? Hopkins might be a link with Welsh poetry, but Dylan denied this specifically. We must accept that he was a word-man, a punster who was sonorous rather than cross-word-puzzlish, and that the individual word or the grouping of words was, until very late in his poetic life, as important, more important, than the total content of what he had to say. And this was certainly true of a good deal of poetry in Welsh.

Without attempting a balance to this complicated equation, I must now turn quickly and finally to my other problem. Dylan returned to Wales, living during the war for a time at New Quay, and later, more permanently at Laugharne, where much of his later work was written in the shed at the top of the Boat House garden. There is one curious and important thing about his location at Laugharne. The English-Welsh linguistic line is strangely broken there: Laugharne is English-speaking, but across the Taf estuary lies the Welsh-speaking countryside of his youthful experience, some of its features visible from the Boat House window. Is it not apparent that this was the perfect way of keeping that memory – that re-remembering, if we recall 'After the Funeral' – unblurred, the physical features in sight and visitable if need be, but the personal and speech impressions unaltered by the overlay of more mature impressions?

However that may be, I must proceed by telescoping my argument. When Dylan came to write the later poems by which most readers now know him, he appeared to have no subject matter except childhood and its memories, the countryside and its 'holy' or sacramental qualities, and death. There is almost nothing about the matter of living as an adult. I would reiterate here Dylan's non-involvement as a child, his failure to become a developing thinker, and his failure to solve his own personal problems, other than poetry, in any meaningful way. What we have in 'In Country Sleep', for instance, is the poet preparing the child – the *child*, mark you–for death:

> Never, my girl, until tolled to sleep by the stern
>
> Bell believe or fear that the rustic shade or spell
> Shall harrow and snow the blood while you ride wide and near,
> For who unmanningly haunts the mountain ravened eaves
> Or skulks in the dell moon but moonshine echoing clear
> From the starred well?
> A hill touches an angel.

What he is saying is that the countryside is clear and sacred. Its tales come from man's imagination: there is no need to be frightened by them. *A hill touches an angel.* Not vice versa. Man is the maker, and he has no need to fear anyone except the Thief, 'meek as the dew' – the stealer-up night by night, Death.

Dylan returned to Wales, then, and did justice, chiefly in his stories, to his childish and youthful memories. But he appeared to have no adult approach to his surroundings. Except, of course – and it's an important *except* – that he sought to come to grips with mortality, which is the most adult problem of all. Nevertheless, the absence of an understanding of other adults, of the community and its rules and intentions, is apparent. Ah! you will say, but what about *Under Milk Wood*? Well, what about *Under Milk Wood*? Let us dismiss immediately any argument as to whether it is a portrait of Laugharne or New Quay. Let us dismiss it as any kind of portrait of a Welsh community. For the first thing to realize, as Walford Davies puts it in his book, *Dylan Thomas*, is that its *ambitions* are *essentially low-key*. It is 'unashamedly a trivializing work in that it reduces a view of life to immediately entertaining details' (pp 68–9). This is not to deny that it is probably the best radio play yet written. But it is meant to be funny and extravagant and poetic, not objective, and the medium lends itself to all these qualities. Raymond Williams gets closer to what I mean when he says (in *Dylan Thomas*, ed. C. B. Cox, p. 97):

> It is not a mature work, but the retained extravagance of an adolescent's imaginings.

I have read arguments (in the work of David Holbrook and Martin Gingerich – the latter in *The Anglo-Welsh Review* No. 49) of the kind of *frustrated love* the characters exhibit – all very serious and high-minded. Surely the one thing that is obvious about the love, from Polly Garter to Mr Waldo to Mrs Dai Bread One and Two, is that it is cynical-adolescent, with its sole pathos reserved for Polly Garter's Little Willy Wee. Mog Edwards, the strictly economic lover residing in Manchester House, is the cub reporter's joke. The Rev. Eli Jenkins, more maturely because restrainedly observed, appears as *eisteddfodwr*, not as minister. Nowhere is there a word to show how the community ticks, what conventions, what aspirations it shows, by what rules it lives. The community is a group of very diverse entertainers who don't live together at all.

What of it, you may argue. That's what Dylan Thomas wanted to write. But in his later poems 'what he wanted to write' was curiously limited. And my contention about *Under Milk Wood* is that he *couldn't* have written the mature, more objective play that a portrait of Laugharne or any other observed community might demand. One piece of evidence at least supports this contention. Dylan originally intended that the play should be called *The Town is Mad*, with Captain Cat being called upon to defend his fellows in court. As the plot unfolded, the prosecuting counsel was to set out the norms of human behaviour, on hearing which the Town would be moved to vote not to defend itself any longer but to accept the label of *Mad*. Dylan abandoned the plot he projected for what seems to me the obvious reason that the presentation of those norms was beyond him. His entry to responsible adult preoccupations was far from certain enough: it was easier to retire upon 'the boy's eye view'.

One of the noticeable features of the text of *Under Milk Wood* is the use of nursery rhymes and children's games, a fact I discovered consciously only when I was called upon to explain parts of it to foreign teachers. Christopher Page, in *The Anglo-Welsh Review* No. 52, shows that the 'clacking scissor-man' from *Struwwelpeter*, the children's storybook that Dylan had read at dame school, appears on many occasions in his earlier poems as the image of castration, unmanning and death. Brian John, in *The Anglo-Welsh Review* No. 51, shows that the 'dilly, dilly . . . Come and be killed' of the loft hawk in 'Over Sir John's Hill', comes straight out of the Victorian nursery rhyme 'Mrs Bond'.

> Oh, what have you got for dinner, Mrs Bond?
> There's beef in the larder and ducks in the pond;
> Dilly, dilly, dilly, dilly, come to be killed,
> For you must be stuffed and my customers filled.

'In Country Sleep' is built upon the nursery tales of Red Riding Hood and Beauty and the Beast. Walford Davies calls 'Poem on his birthday' an 'assertion of innocence in the face of ideological blankness' (*ibid.*, p. 81). The direction of my arguments is, I trust, becoming clearer. I am seeking to suggest that in his last poems Dylan Thomas faced death certain only of the equipment of a child and that the pastoral scene of Laugharne was the sacramental covert in which he waited for it. Or, to put it another way, that, life having given him as an adult neither satisfaction nor mastery, he had retired upon the imagination – not in the still-determined, shaping manner of Wallace Stevens, but recessively, into what could still be recaptured of the child's wonder at the natural world and his innocent population of the mind.

Much of what I have written here has, I am aware, been put crudely and sketchily, and not solely for lack of space. It is an argument that needs deeper consideration and a great deal more textual flesh. But I have been moved to write it not by any erudite psychological perception so much as an instinct more literary in genesis, if not yet precise and fully knowledgeable. The issue, for me, is not whether 'Over Sir John's Hill' is the finest poem in English of its decade – there is no dispute over the continuance, even the perfection, of Dylan Thomas's technical gifts – but whether this poem, together with 'Fern Hill', 'Holy Spring', 'In Country Sleep', 'A Winter's Tale' and 'Poem on his birthday', do not demonstrate such a narrowing and closing of poetic interest that the end is clearly foreshadowed. And that that end has a closer connection than is commonly appreciated with much of what happened at his beginning – this I believe too. His Laugharne was the only morsel of Wales he had really made his own.

Poetry Wales

Poems from Books

Dannie Abse **Peachstone**

I do not visit his grave. He is not there.
Out of hearing, out of reach. I miss him here,
seeing hair grease at the back of a chair
near a firegrate where his spit sizzled,
or noting, in the cut-glass bowl, a peach.

For that night his wife brought him a peach,
his favourite fruit, while the sick light glowed,
and his slack, dry mouth sucked, sucked, sucked,
with dying eyes closed – perhaps for her sake –
till bright as blood the peachstone showed.

Funland and Other Poems, Hutchinson

Dannie Abse **Car Journeys**

1 *Down the M4*
Me! dutiful son going back to South Wales, this
time afraid
to hear my mother's news. Too often, now, her
friends are disrobed,
and my aunts and uncles, too, go into the hole,
one by one.
The beautiful face of my mother is in its ninth
decade.

Each visit she tells me the monotonous story of
clocks.
'Oh dear,' I say, or 'how funny,' till I feel my hair
turning grey
for I've heard that perishable one two hundred
times before –
like the rugby 'amateurs' with golden sovereigns
in their socks.

Then the Tawe ran fluent and trout-coloured over
stones stonier,
more genuine; then Annabella, my mother's
mother, spoke Welsh
with such an accent the village said, 'Tell the
truth, fach,
you're no Jewess. *They're* from the Bible. *You're*
from Patagonia!'

I'm driving down the M4 again under bridges that
leap
over me then shrink in my side mirror. Ystalyfera
is farther
than smoke and God further than all distance
known. I whistle
no hymn but an old Yiddish tune my mother
knows. It won't keep.

2 *Incident on a summer night*

The route not even in the A.A. book.
I'm nowhere, I thought, driving slowly
because of the raw surface of the lane
that developed between converging hedges;
then, soon, fabulous in the ghastly wash
of headlights, a naked man approached
crying without inhibition, one hand to his face,
his somehow familiar mouth agape.

Surely he could see me?
From the two moth-filled headlights
surely he would draw back, change his pace?
This road to Paradise, I muttered.
At last I passed him or say, rather, he passed me.
Afterwards, the accelerating lane widened
and long lights fumbled, momentarily,
hedges, hurtling gate, country wall, amazing tree.

And they, too, seem like images from sleep:
this Asian child and shadow
playing on a rubbish heap;
that old man incognito
preaching to the pigeons.
'Kill the Reds,' he says, 'kill the Reds.'
I wind up the car window.

Nearby, sunlight on a broken bottle
throws trinket colours on a stone,
but the ancient man in smoked glasses
walks to the right alone
mouthing a forgotten language,
walks out of sight, off the page.

And I? I leave the car, feel dizzy –
even the plastic seating's hot.
Grounded pigeons purr their gutturals,
the pistons in their heads are busy.
When the door slams its small shot
the pigeons reach for the sky,
the shadow chases the child.

In Hotel Insomnia, once, at dawn,
I thought I heard those pigeons' wings
whirring outside my numbered door.
It was only the lift gone wild.
Up and down on a nightmare ride
its gates opened at each floor,
gates of ivory or of horn:
no Asian child, nor ancient man,
nobody at all inside.

4 *Driving home*

Opposing carbeams wash my face.
Such flickerings hypnotize. To keep awake
I listen to the B.B.C. through cracklings
of static, fade-outs under bridges,
to a cool expert who, in lower case,
computes and graphs 'the ecological
disasters that confront the human race'.

Almost immediately (ironically?),
I see blue flashing lights ahead and brake
before a car accordioned, floodlit, men heaving
at a stretcher, an ambulance oddly angled, tame,
  in wait.
Afterwards, silent, I drive home cautiously
where, late, the eyes of my youngest child
flicker dreamily, and are full of television.

'He's waited up,' his mother says, 'to say
  goodnight.'
My son smiles briefly. Such emotion! I surprise
myself and him when I hug him tight.

Funland and Other Poems, Hutchinson

Edwin Brock **Prototypes**

1.

King George the Fifth
looked like my grandfather
and felt as close

when he died
I walked the streets
staring at houses

and their faces
to see if people
looked the same and

their homes still stood.
For a week
we were on the brink

of war or an earthquake
and when my mother
laughed at me

I abandoned her
to God's anger
or soldiers from the Tower.

King George the Fifth
was my first and last
king, his children

and their children
were never properly introduced
and I ignored them.

2.

My father played the piano
with one finger of his right hand
and the fist of his left

he laughed at Gracie Fields
Max Miller and was away from home
for weeks at a time

when he died I cried
for my mother
and forgot.

I have never mastered the art
of becoming my father:
I have three children

pale jackets, suede shoes
and laugh at comedians
I do not admire

I stay away from home
for weeks at a time
but I do not resemble him

when he came home
he brought himself with him
and sat down

when I arrive
I hit the piano with both hands
and nothing happens.

3.

Britannia glowed
from Empire Day
all the way to Barry Road

a big-girl jumped over
her skipping rope
and walked away on her hands

on Saturday night
I jumped over a saxophone
and ran among mad skirts

by Sunday I had married
the girl next door and all the saxophones
played the Last Post.

4.

On my bedside table
is a triptych
of a king, a father and a wife

at night I sleep
with one eye open
hoping to surprise them

I am wrong:
their dead faces
fill all my gaps

and nothing happens
except I contain them,
father-king and dancing wife

they have killed my ear
for saxophones
and nobody, not even

Fred Astaire, could take
his toes to a brass band
playing a requiem mass.

The Portraits and The Poses, Secker & Warburg

Michael Burn **Exempted**

She sits in front of her glass,
Leaning her cheek on her hand, a little morose,
And says, 'My lines are all going downwards.'
She does not know what I know
Of the compact of Time with Beauty . . .
To continue his task, the part he cannot evade,
And yet to concede
For this exceptional one, not as a precedent,
Since lines must come, come then as a setting for
jewels,
Or faint as the gossamer lines
On a perfectly mended bowl;
Since the body's strength must grow less, then to
pass
Into the spirit, the soul,
And to show
In the eyes, that may glitter no more, but shall
glow

So she sits in front of her glass,
Takes off her make-up, ties her hair,
And comes to bed,

Little knowing she has been watching a miracle.

Out on a Limb, Chatto & Windus

Michael Burn **Please!**

O God, do something worldly for us!
O, load us with a very large sum of money
Now,
And in any reliable currency
Allow
Us to be surprised. Fill up our dustbin
With packages of undevalued
Yen,
Reichsmark, or the more humbly pursued
Pound.
Begin
Each day with the
Sound
Of a not small cheque.
Let
Paul Get-
-ty and Barbara Hutton take a fancy to either or
both of us.
Thrus-
-t several remunerative and gay
Tempta-
-tions in our way,
Such as a
Venice palazzo with a whale-
-scale swimpool, and a
Merc,
Or two Mercs. Arrange for my
Work
To be high-
-ly app-
-lauded everywhere, and re-
-warded beyond its merits. Snap
Thy magnificent fingers, be
Not skimping with largesse,
Tax-free;
For example gold

Francs,
And from untold
Swiss rolls and credits in countless
Banks,
O God, withhold
Not
O not withhold Thy hand.
But
With such mundane meaningless things,
  Almighty, cover us thick
Ageing babes in-the-wood, and
Cover us quick!

Out on a Limb, Chatto & Windus

Conleth Ellis **A Question of Style**

See where my splay-footed starling mulls
Ungainly across the lawn, stooped over
Like an old woman peering for windfalls,
Trusting to luck: his searching, haphazard
As a half-blind hen's in an empty haggard,
Could hardly be called an earnest endeavour.

Now, here's my elegant blackbird, deft,
With mannequin posture, neat, debonair;
His sensitive feet are stethoscopes pressed
To the earthworm's heartbeat. 'Please, allow
Me to show you how this is done.' He bows,
A pleasure to watch, methodical, sure.

Still, starling families manage to live;
And blackbirds, for all their superior skills,
Have nothing to teach them on how to survive:
Both have time to take time off for singing,
And in the end differ only in bringing
To living their equally eloquent styles.

Under the Stone, Gill & Macmillan, Dublin

Conleth Ellis **A Memory**

Barney Hennessy terrified me,
Coming to the pump with his bucket,
Talking to himself or shouting
At no one in particular.

A plate in his head they said
He had brought back from the war,
And the thought of that frightened
Me more than his muttering,

For I pictured clearly
Whenever he limped past
A dull tin plate like the one
My mother made tarts on.

Though others said it was gold,
I couldn't imagine it shining
Inside his head like the nib
Of a pen or a watch

Or a wedding ring. More likely tin.
And my teeth watered with pain
At the ring of his galvanised pail
On the foot of the stuttering pump.

Under the Stone, Gill & Macmillan, Dublin

Ruth Fainlight **Lilith**

Lilith, Adam's first companion,
Assumed her equality.
For this she was banished.

God had created her
From the same earth as Adam.
She stood her ground, amazed
By the idea of differences.

Adam and God were embarrassed,
Humiliated. It was true—
They had been formed
At the same time, the two
Halves of His reflection.

Her expectations
Should have seemed justified.
But Adam needed to understand God.
A creature must now worship him,
Constrained and resentful
As he was. God encouraged him.

To guard His mystery, God
Caused Adam to swoon. There, when he awoke,
Awaited Eve, the chattel.

Eyes downcast, his phallus
The first thing she noticed.
The snake reminded her of it.
Easy to equate the two.

That nagging ache in his side
Where the rib was extracted
(In memory of which
The soldier thrust his spear)
Keeps Adam irritable.

Lilith's disgrace thus defined
Good and evil. She would be
Outside, the feared, the alien,
Hungry and dangerous.
His seed and Eve's fruit
At hazard from her rage.

Good wives make amulets
Against her, to protect themselves.
Lilith is jealous.

The Region's Violence, Hutchinson

J. C. Hall **A Burning**

The morning she brought the package down and said
'Please burn them,' I only hope my huge surprise
Didn't appear or make her feel ashamed
That now at last (or so it seemed) her grief
Had so digested every word and phrase
That to thumb through his letters still became
A dry indulgence. Laying aside my book
I took her sacrifice without a word.
'You don't mind, do you?' – I shook my head,
Not sure whether I minded but sure at least
That what I did and how I did it then
Meant, for us both, an end. I took them down –
Two hundred perhaps, all neatly tied, the news
Of school and barrack room, of how he'd come
Third in the class one week, and later found
Canada, where he trained, a friendly place,
And how after the war they'd take a cruise –
Took them behind the greenhouse out of sight
And shook them out like leaves. I doubt she saw
Anything of the blaze, and the thin smoke
Blew low over the hedge and scudded away
Down the valley. Some wouldn't catch. I raked
And prodded them with a fierce tenderness,
Coaxing his care to rest. For still his hand
Curled in the heat and words like negatives
Briefly stood out more boldly – his memory etched
On feathery fronds one moment, then breaking up
In fragile ruin.
                                        And when at last
Nothing but ash remained, I threw on earth
Like coffin-scatter, put back the hoe, went in
The kitchen way where, sharpening a knife,
She looked up, half-dismayed. I nodded, said
'They're gone,' matter-of-fact, and sat to eat
Whatever she'd cooked to keep us both alive.

A House of Voices, Chatto & Windus

J. C. Hall **Persons Once Loved**

Persons once loved are loved in a sense always.
They go yet never depart. Their times are driven
So deep we keep the occasions, like birthdays
That come round year after year though nothing's
given.

Four or five women have cut their names in my
heart.
Remembering one's not disloyal to the others.
The paradox is, however much they've hurt,
Or we've hurt them, they're still in a way our lovers.

Impossible not to wonder how they are
Or who they're with or whether our fashions linger
In what they do – like the ache of a limb not there
Or a wedding ring stuck fast on a widowed finger.

A House of Voices, Chatto & Windus

Michael Hamburger **Memory**

My wives do not write.
Sweetly young, hair flowing,
They walk where they belong,
Riverside, lakeside,
Mountainside, hillside,
Woodland or grassy plain.

One I consoled –
Black-haired, sad
In her forest clearing –
Another I followed
From a wellspring up in the scree
To a pool's golden rushes.

Did I leave them, forsake them?
I travelled,
Remember no parting.
Ways, I recall, transitions,
The shadows, the colours turning,
Herbs acrid or heady,
Sweet wives the world over,
Sweet virgins walking where they belong –

Unchanged, unchanging regions,
And they unchanged.

But by the knee a stranger
Clawed me, held on;
I fought: my grappling hand
Slid deep into rotten flesh,
A hole behind his ear.
I knocked him down and ran,
Clegs covering me,

A grey crust;
Ran to the church, thinking
They could not enter there,
But still they clung, stinging,
And up I climbed, climbed
To the belfry, pursued
By a man half-decayed.

Sweet wives, sweet virgins
Walk still unchanged,
Do not write, do not miss me,
Never forget.
It was the sunshine, the shadows,
It was the herbs and the haze.

Ownerless Earth, Carcanet

Treblinka

A Survivor Speaks:

That winter night they were burning corpses
And from the bonfire, flooding the whole camp
Flared purple and blue and red and orange and gold,
The many colours of Joseph's coat, who was chosen.
Not cold for once we at the barrack windows
Blinked and listened; the opera singer,
Unafraid for once, found his full voice and gave it
To words, to a music that gushed like blood from a
 wound:
Eli, Eli . . . his question too in whose name
Long we'd been dirt to be wiped off, dust to be
 dispersed –
Older than he, old as the silence of God.
In that light we knew it; and the complaint was
 praise,

Was thankfulness for death, the lost and the
promised land,
The gathering up at last, all our hundred hues
Fierce in one radiance gathered by greater darkness,
The darkness that took our kings, David and
Solomon
Who living had burnt with the same fire;
All our hundred languages gathered again in one
silence.

To live was the law; though to live – and not only
here –
Was a hundred times over to spit in our own faces,
Wipe ourselves out of creation, scatter as dust,
Eat grass, and the dung that feeds grass.
The grass, the dung, the spittle – here we saw them
consumed,
Even these bodies fit in the end to yield light.

Back in a room in a house in a street in a town
I forget the figures, remember little but this:
That to live is not good enough: everything,
anything
Proved good enough for life – there, and not only
there.
Yet we lived, a few of us, perhaps with no need but
this:
To tell of the fire in the night and briefly flare like the
dead.

Ownerless Earth, Carcanet

Michael Longley **A Nativity**

Dog

He will be welcome to
His place in the manger –

Anaesthetist and surgeon
Muffling the child's cries

And biting through the cord
That joins God to Mary.

She-goat

A protective midwife –
She roots out with her horns

A sour cake from the straw
And, jaws grinding sideways,

Devours the afterbirth
Of the child of heaven.

Bullocks

They will make a present
Of their empty purses –

Their perfected music
An interval between

The man with the scissors
And the man with the knife.

Bullfinch

Slipped in by an old master
At the edge of the picture –

An idea in Mary's head,
A splash of colour –

Thistle-tweaker, theologian,
Eater-of-thorns.

An Exploded View, Gollancz

George Macbeth **To the Autumn**

Through barren trees
Each Sunday, as this long November slows,
I age across the park. Where puddles freeze,
The oaks crust silver, and a sycamore snows

Leaves in the ride,
Though no tree feels the death-white mist and wind
As clammy as I do, through fleece and hide.
That clay-stiff wind! I loathe it, and feel pinned

Into my pale
On the slopes of forty, though unreconciled
To a squirrel ageing, even to a snail.
The dank force masses, but the air is mild.

Somewhere, a breath
Of delicate festering, a sort of stew
Spirals, to taint the breeze. I breathe my death,
Dreaming of being born again, made new

By power and art,
And losing solid matter, like soiled clay
Off mouldering football-boots. I want to start
Fresh from the sloughings, free from all decay,

Light as a fly
In crisp October, when the final few
Shake out their wings, believing the rich dye
Will never fade, and brilliant in their blue.

At the door of birth
I pause, and count those left: the ones with tails
And iridescent glister, shot from earth
In Aztec richness, as their season ails.

They arc, and shine
Over the water, turquoise as they burn.
I am born with them, and make their fury mine,
Savaging the chill air. Silent, I turn

Where fire recedes
Across the river, as the sun declines.
I see the last one founder by the reeds.
Up from the mud, a grey dung-beetle whines.

A Poet's Year, Gollancz

Norman MacCaig **Behind a Shut Door**

I see a stone.
It makes a building, I see it rise
From a cloud of earth to its own invented skies.

I know a man –
A winding column of refugees
From the past, bowed under his chattel of centuries.

I hear a bird,
And testaments in a cage of song
Cry cruel love; they sigh and cry How long?

I watch a child
Whose weeping is all there is. I say Yes,
Yes, yes to that terrible loneliness.

I take no heed –
A crime that every day I commit
And hate and hate myself because of it.

The White Bird, Chatto & Windus

Alasdair Maclean **Our Bull**

He has the slimmest hips
and the most massive shoulders.
Viewed from the front
he's the width of a whole field.

His kingdom is red-rimmed.
Everything that moves in it he stops.
Everything that's stopped he moves.

Pressure builds up in him periodically.
His sides heave and quiver.
Jets of steam gush from his nostrils.
One more pound per square inch
and he'd explode.

Even at rest in the long grass
he's still a metaphor for danger:
the round black hump of his back,
horn tips rising over it,
bobs menacingly in the green swell.

Standing he dominates the landscape.
Tourists sweat their way past him
at fifty yards or more,
feeling with outstretched toes
for the next foothold.
The women say nothing;
a tendency to dawdle
when almost safe
reveals the difference
between the fear they'd own to
and the one they hide.

No blame to them.
He moves from legend to reality with ease
and brings the best part of his story with him.
His bellowing is preliminary only. He delivers.

Yet he will follow a cow
about to come in heat
so modestly he seems to shrink.
He accepts her insults meekly
and keeps his weapon sheathed.
One thrust through the vitals pays for all.

Or in a randy mood, no cows available,
he'll stab the air, semen dripping from him

in the ambiguous prodigality of nature.
Our bull is state-owned
and will be savaged by and by.
Someone in an office somewhere
charts his progress.
Calf production is plotted against time
and the curve goes down.

I was given once
the chance to watch a bull,
his services all done,
being poleaxed in a slaughterhouse.
He died so quickly and so heavily
I trembled.
Before my heart
had ceased to register the shock
he was chained and swung,
a bucket hung from his horns
and his throat tapped.

From the Wilderness, Gollancz

Alasdair Maclean

Tallyman

It must be easily
the hottest day so far this year.
Along the crest of the Glendryan Hills
the grass snaps under my feet.
If it were dark the rocks would glow.

I see the flies and hear them
before I see the sheep they quarrel over.
A cloud of bluebottles
thick enough to cast a shadow.
When she moves off at my approach
they rev up and follow.

Maggots, of course. You could scoop them
off her back in handfuls.
Small carnivorous worms with non-stop appetites,
they worry her to death.
The flies wait for the bones.

Sheep die unnoticed as a rule.
I was lucky to come across this one.
They go apart when their time comes
but without knowing why. They die instinctively.

I fan myself with my notebook.
It was cooler after all at sea level.
A stray bluebottle
follows me persistently all the way down.

From the Wilderness, Gollancz

Alasdair Maclean

Death of an Old Woman

She lived too much alone to be aware of it,
in a cottage on a stretch of moor,
built before the distant road was built
and shunned by everything built since.
Her croft had faded through the years
for lack of drainage and proper food,
bled of its green until the eye
could hardly tell where it began or ended.
Her house had a hole in the thatch
to let the smoke out – when there was any –
and the rain in, and three small openings
in the walls, two for light and one for charity,
and all about the size she was accustomed to.
The man who found her dead was drawn
in that direction by the movement.
That was the door of her empty henhouse
flapping in the wind, a nerve continuing to twitch.

She herself was lying in her bed,
causing a slight ripple in the blankets.
She had an English Bible in her hands,
upside down. The doctor who examined her
stated that her mouth was full of raw potato.

From the Wilderness, Gollancz

Edwin Morgan **Hyena**

I am waiting for you.
I have been travelling all morning through the bush
and not eaten.
I am lying at the edge of the bush
on a dusty path that leads from the burnt-out kraal.
I am panting, it is midday, I found no water-hole.
I am very fierce without food and although my eyes
are screwed to slits against the sun
you must believe I am prepared to spring.

What do you think of me?
I have a rough coat like Africa.
I am crafty with dark spots
like the bush-tufted plains of Africa.
I sprawl as a shaggy bundle of gathered energy
like Africa sprawling in its waters.
I trot, I lope, I slaver, I am a ranger.
I hunch my shoulders. I eat the dead.

Do you like my song?
When the moon pours hard and cold on the veldt
I sing, and I am the slave of darkness.
Over the stone walls and the mud walls and the
 ruined places
and the owls, the moonlight falls.
I sniff a broken drum. I bristle. My pelt is silver.
I howl my song to the moon – up it goes.
Would you meet me there in the waste places?

It is said I am a good match
for a dead lion. I put my muzzle
at his golden flanks, and tear. He
is my golden supper, but my tastes are easy.
I have a crowd of fangs, and I use them.
Oh and my tongue – do you like me
when it comes lolling out over my jaw

very long, and I am laughing?
I am not laughing.
But I am not snarling either, only
panting in the sun, showing you
what I grip
carrion with.

I am waiting
for the foot to slide,
for the heart to seize,
for the leaping sinews to go slack,
for the fight to the death to be fought to the death,
for a glazing eye and the rumour of blood.
I am crouching in my dry shadows
till you are ready for me.
My place is to pick you clean
and leave your bones to the wind.

From Glasgow to Saturn, Carcanet

Leslie Norris **Bridges**

Imagine the bridge launched, its one foot
Clamped hard on bedrock, and such grace
In its growth it resembles flying, is flight
Almost. It is not chance when they speak
Of throwing a bridge; it leaves behind a track
Of its parallel rise and fall, solid
In quarried stone, in timber, in milled
Alloy under stress. A bridge is

The path of flight. A friend, a soldier,
Built a laughable wartime bridge over
Some unknown river. In featureless night
He threw from each slid bank the images
Of his crossing, working in whispers, under
Failing lamps. As they built, braced spars,
Bolted taut the great steel plugs, he hoped
His bridge would stand in brawny daylight, complete,

The two halves miraculously knit. But
It didn't. Airily they floated above
Midstream, going nowhere, separate
Beginnings of different bridges, offering
The policies of inaction, neither coming
Nor going. His rough men cursed, sloped off,
Forded quite easily a mile lower.
It was shallow enough for his Land Rover.

I have a bridge over a stream. Four
Wooden sleepers, simple, direct. After rain,
Very slippery. I rarely cross right over,
Preferring to stand, watching the grain
On running water. I like such bridges best,
River bridges on which men always stand,
In quiet places. Unless I could have that other,
A bridge launched, hovering, wondering where to
land.

Mountains Polecats Pheasants, Chatto & Windus

John Ormond **Cathedral Builders**

They climbed on sketchy ladders towards God,
With winch and pulley hoisted hewn rock into
  heaven,
Inhabited sky with hammers, defied gravity,
Deified stone, took up God's house to meet Him,

And came down to their suppers and small beer;
Every night slept, lay with their smelly wives,
Quarrelled and cuffed the children, lied,
Spat, sang, were happy or unhappy,

And every day took to the ladders again;
Impeded the rights of way of another summer's
Swallows, grew greyer, shakier, became less inclined
To fix a neighbour's roof of a fine evening,

Saw naves sprout arches, clerestories soar,
Cursed the loud fancy glaziers for their luck,
Somehow escaped the plague, got rheumatism,
Decided it was time to give it up,

To leave the spire to others; stood in the crowd
Well back from the vestments at the consecration,
Envied the fat bishop his warm boots,
Cocked up a squint eye and said, 'I bloody did that.'

Definition of a Waterfall, Oxford University Press

John Ormond

Letter to a Geologist

for Wynn Williams

When was it we last met? When the stag
Devoured the vivid serpent then wept
Jewels as tears, antidote to all poisons.

Or so it seems to me. You write
Of your November find, fossil coral
Within a spit of that house of yours

(Which is too far from me. The free hold
Of our friendship is at stake); the coral,
Bring me a piece of it, bring it soon.

I would place it with that other handful
Torn, only last year, from a living reef
Six thousand miles away in the Indian Ocean;

And, in the pairing, see what you deduce:
That once your Flintshire hill – for me as distant
As the Seychelles themselves – was tropical.

The shifting land you've shown me: off-shore
Islands in green counties; tide-ways
500 million years of age under the plough;

And desert sands stranded in river-cliffs
On Deeside, come from the Sahara.
If these could move, could not *you* move, too?

Come south. Ferns in grey shale speak of you
From my shelf, of coal measures we were both
Born on. Your nugget of fool's gold

Is paperweight over the dross of my draft poems.
I know that, as I greet you, mountains shrink
Or inch up; the sea-kings' beds are unmade;

But these are rustlings, mere cosmic sighs
Unheard beneath our breathing. Let us tell
Some part of earth's true time together soon

With a drink, a song – the lullabies you sang
My children, come sing them again before sleep;
Let us say to each other words of a common world.

I've grown too solemn, so recall your jest
Of Man's not really falling off the peg
Vertical, ready-made, in Genesis:

But should you, in the field, come upon Moses
Striding through cloud on a Snowdonian height
With new or adjusted Tablets of the Law

Please check the Lord's amendments
Before you raise your hammer to opine
What stone it is that they are carved upon.

Yours, as the mountains move,
Love, ever,
John

Definition of a Waterfall, Oxford University Press

Peter Porter **James Joyce Sings 'Il Mio Tesoro'**

Something to warm your back teeth
even if your shirt's making its presence felt,
some piece of calculated impertinence –

My theory about *Hamlet* can drop
until I get these divisions right,
I mean the way McCormack gets them:
che sol di stragi e morti
nunzio voglio tornar
The Peace of the Fathers be with you
and all the browning photographs of Europe

Among the clean mountains the mad
are trained like roses on a trellis
                              pruned for love

My books are easier to write than read
and by God that's the proper division of labour

Nobody but me has produced literature
as great as music
                              (I make an exception
of the author of *Hamlet*)

Do I hear some ijjit asking about
Proust and Synge and Pound
                              and a lot of names
I think I saw on raisin packets?

A fine tenor voice
the peace of great art

I never knew when to stop

If I'd been christened Stanislaus
I'd have claimed the throne of Poland

A Share of the Market, Ulsterman Publications

Vernon Scannell **Sleeping Beauty**

It was evening when he reached the place.
Outside, the air was motionless.
He listened for the sound of sigh or snore.
Silence trickled down his face;
He touched his sword for confidence,
Then parted the dark foliage at the door.

He entered. She was beautiful.
He pressed his mouth to hers; her lips
Grew warm and parted, breathing quick yet deep;
Her waking welcome magical,
Until her sharp teeth came to grips
And munched; for she was starved from that long
sleep.

The Winter Man, Allison & Busby

John Smith **Death at the Opera**

Is this what death is like? I sit
Dressed elegantly in black and white, in an
  expensive seat,
Watching Violetta expire in Covent Garden.
How beautiful she is! As her voice lures me toward
  her death
The strings of the orchestra moisten my eyes with
  tears,
Though the tenor is too loud. Is this what death is
  like?
No one moves. Violetta coughs; stumbles toward the
  bed.
Twenty miles away in the country my father is dying.
Violetta catches at her throat. Let me repeat: my
  father
Is dying in a semi-detached house on a main road
Twenty miles off in the country. The skull is visible.

I do not want it to end. How exquisitely moving is
  death,
The approach to it. The lovers sob. Soon they will be
  wrenched apart.
How romantic it all is. Her hand is a white moth
Fluttering against the coverlet of the bed. The bones
Of my father's hands poke through his dry skin.
His eyes look into a vacancy of space. He spits into
  a cup.
In a few moments now Violetta will give up the
  ghost;
The doctor, the maid, the tenor who does not love
  her, will sob.
Almost, our hearts will stop beating. How refreshed
  we have been.
My father's clothes, too large for his shrunken frame,
Make him look like a parcel. Ah! The plush curtains
  are opening.

The applause! The applause! It drowns out the ugly
noise
Of my father's choking and spitting. The bright lights
Glitter far more than the hundred watt bulb at home.
Dear Violetta! How she enjoys the flowers, like
wreathes,
Showered for her own death. She gathers them to
her.
We have avoided the coffin. I think that my father
Would like a box of good plain beech, being a man
From Buckinghamshire, a man of the country, a man
of the soil.
I have seen my father, who is fond of animals, kill a
cat
That was old and in pain with a blow from the edge
of his palm.
He buried it in the garden, but I cannot remember
its name.

Now the watchers are dispersing; the taxis drive
away
Black in the black night. A huddle of people wait
Like mourners round the stage door. Is this what
death is like?
For Violetta died after all. It is merely a ghost,
The voice gone, the beautiful dress removed, who
steps in the rain.
Art, I conceive, is not so removed from life; for we
look at death
Whether real or imagined, from an impossible
distance
And somewhere a final curtain is always descending.
The critics are already phoning their obituaries to
the papers.
I do not think God is concerned with such trivial
matters
But, father, though there will be no applause, die
well.

Entering Rooms, Chatto & Windus

 Eels

With the colliers out a week now
the Taff at Rhydfelen is deep and as green
as my father says it's ever been,
and boys on the bridge, like I was once, throw
lines into the fast stream below.

Many's the time I stood by there
as the river slid with its load of small coal
past our village, over the weir,
all silver and smooth as a mole.
I'm wondering what our barbed ambitions were –

the pike with sovereign scales,
perhaps, or even the most venerable salmon
that swam in the legendary pools of Wales?
Fact is, nothing was ever won
by our bent pin and penny bun

from such poor water; except
during the troubles there were always eels –
those brazen scavengers kept
us in full summer's sport as up they leapt
from the coiled darkness towards our reels,

and we felt the spun blood's
principalities generating through our rods
as the monsters, hugely fanged,
writhed in their long agonies. I understand
why, at last, like stripling gods

we would decapitate the devils:
they came to the cwm when times were slack,
the factory's gate and the foundry's stack
beset by their seething evils.
At school we used to paint our rivers black,

blue was for the sky and sea.
I remember that on the bridge at Rhydfelen,
hoping the boys will not see
this landed man's ferocity
as he turns to smash those wicked heads in.

Exiles All, Christopher Davies

Meic Stephens

Hooters

Night after night from my small bed
I heard the hooters blowing up and down the cwm:
Lewis Merthyr, Albion, Nantgarw, Ty-draw –
these were the familiar banshees of my boyhood.

For each shift they hooted, not a night
without the high moan that kept me from sleep;
often, as my father beyond the thin wall
rumbled like the turbines he drove at work, I

stood for hours by the box-room window,
listening. The dogs of Annwn barked for me then,
Trystan called without hope to Esyllt
across the black waters. Ai, it was their wail

I heard that night a Heinkel flew up
the Taff and its last bomb fell on our village;
we huddled under the cwtsh, making
beasts against the candle's light until the sky

was clear once more, and the hooters
sounded. I remember too how their special din
brought ambulances to the pit yard,
the masked men coming up the shaft with corpses

gutted by fire; then, as the big cars
moved down the blinded row on the way to Glyntaf,
all the hooters for twenty miles about
began to swell, a great hymn grieving the heart.

Years ago that was. I had forgotten
the hooters: my disasters, these days, are less
spectacular. We live now in this city:
our house is large, detached and behind fences.

I sleep easily, but waking tonight
found the same desolate clangour in my ears
that from an old and sunken level
used to chill me as a boy – the inevitable hooter

that paralyses with its mute alarm.
How long I have been standing at this window,
a man in the grown dark, only my wife
knows as I make for her white side, shivering.

Exiles All, Christopher Davies

Anthony Thwaite **The Bonfire**

Day by day, day after day, we fed it
With straw, mown grass, shavings, shaken weeds,
The huge flat leaves of umbrella plants, old spoil
Left by the builders, combustible; yet it
Coughed fitfully at the touch of a match,
Flared briefly, spat flame through a few dry seeds
Like a chain of fireworks, then slumped back to the
soil
Smouldering and smoky, leaving us to watch

Only a heavy grey mantle without fire.
This glum construction seemed choked at heart,
The coils of newspaper burrowed into its hulk
Led our small flames into the middle of nowhere,
Never touching its centre, sodden with rot.
Ritual petrol sprinklings wouldn't make it start
But swerved and vanished over its squat brown bulk,
Still heavily sullen, grimly determined not

To do away with itself. A whiff of smoke
Hung over it as over a volcano.
Until one night, late, when we heard outside
A crackling roar, and saw the far field look
Like a Gehenna claiming its due dead.
The beacon beckoned, fierily aglow
With days of waiting, hiding deep inside
Its bided time, ravenous to be fed.

Inscriptions, Oxford University Press

Ted Walker **New Forest Ponies**

They stopped from a gallop. Steam
left them like epiphanies
loose in the dusk. I saw them
whisking at snowflakes like flies.

It was a pair of forest
mares, briskets slung like hammocks
of fat matelots. With rapt lust
they browsed remnants of picnics

beside the Brockenhurst road.
Hobos, they rifled litter-bins,
turfing out chicken bones; then stood
casually among beer-cans,

posed for a snapshot album.
I nudged them along the verge
until their stallion came
prancing a disremembered rage

through the ice twilight. His strength
was flagged, a softening thong
of wash-leather. The cushy south
where he lives, where I belong,

would paddock him for gymkhanas,
currying his fourteen hands
to a genteel handsomeness.
Now he smelt like failing ponds,

shut cinemas. He began to come
at me. Gripping the fence-post,
I waited. But he ambled, a tame
elderly man in tweeds, lost

in some reverie of war,
all wildness shrunk. White of eyes
was mush, the shown teeth sulphur
dull. He let me feel him – thews,

veins, worn cordage to the touch.
I held him grass on my palm.
He cadged himself a sandwich;
mooched away, slavering jam.

Gloves to the Hangman, Cape

Ted Walker

The Emigrés

Visiting from Britain, I take my ease
In a Massachusetts yard. Willows
Have opened overnight along the ridge;
This is the second spring I've seen this year.

I watch as my once-English hostess
Moves across the shadow of the spruces
At her door. She calls her home a cottage
And puts on homeliness like a sweater.

She's tried, over and over, to grow grass
Around the place; grass, and a few roses,
And even, look, a bit of privet hedge
To remind her of home in Warwickshire.

She brings me bourbon in an ice-packed glass
And tinkles on about the neighbours' houses.
Americanisms glint like a badge
Pinned onto her. She much prefers life here,

She protests, remembering what life was
For her in England – the dirt, rising prices,
Always having to live at the edge
Of her nerves. Not to mention the weather.

I stir my drink. 'I'd not mind it either,
For a while,' I say. Martins lodge,
Like my swallows at home, in crevices
Of her roof. 'Oh, purple martins, those

Damn things. I'll have to rake them down from
there,'
She says. 'Mind you, it's not that I begrudge
Them somewhere to live. But if you saw the mess
They make, you wouldn't think me heartless.'

Now, in his office near a fall-out shelter
High over downtown Boston, husband Reg
Will be turning his calendar (English Views
In Summertime) into May. The two of us,

Last evening, swept the last of the winter
Cones into a heap. Outside his garage
Afterwards, he told me, watching the flames,
Of all his new, perpetual worries:

There's his job – they daren't have kids. And Russia.
And how he'll never keep up with the mortgage.
Not to mention the droughts, the six-foot snows,
In the yard where nothing English ever grows.

Gloves to the Hangman, Cape

Points of View

Anthony Thwaite **The Two Poetries**

I had a dream recently which seemed to show some anxiety symptoms. A television pundit (he had the sort of presence John Berger has, but I don't think that's relevant) was analysing a painting for our benefit, and as he did so the painting kept on changing, undergoing a metamorphosis to suit the pundit's interpretation. 'Looked at in another way,' the slightly bored voice insisted – and immediately the features of the painting blurred, changed and fell into an entirely different focus. 'The face in the bottom left-hand corner,' the voice would begin, and as the words went on the face assumed the features the critic attributed to it. Everything was in a state of flux; nothing would stay still. I woke up bewildered, afraid and unsure of my bearings.

But even as I woke, I realized that the dream wasn't just arbitrary and meaningless. It had something to do with my unhappiness about the way in which art is regarded today, and I could see that (as so often in dreams) though the dream was about a painting, there'd been a transference from the art that concerns me most: poetry. Before my dream, I'd just been reading the tenth anniversary issue of Ian Hamilton's fierce little magazine, *the Review*, in which 35 poets and critics discussed the present state of poetry and its future prospects. Perhaps I'd read too much of the magazine at one sitting, and was suffering from mental indigestion, even nausea: dreams can begin that way.

Yet I can see that the roots go further back than that. A few months ago a friend of mine, a Cambridge English don, was talking to me about what he half-jokingly called 'naive reading': this was something he said had been lost and ought to be brought back. We'd grown so used to the idea of complexity in literature, to ferreting out ambiguities and measuring levels, that we'd lost the knack of straightforward reading. And our ingenuities actually get in the way of noticing this, of being plain about plain matters, so that (my friend said) students reading for the English Tripos often seemed incapable of responding to simplicities but forced themselves into reading obliquely.

At first this may seem odd. We're so often told that students today respond most readily and enthusiastically to the instant simplicities of, for example, Rod McKuen, Leonard Cohen and Roger McGough. Here's a quotation from Patricia Beer's contribution to the *Review* questionnaire:

> My experience as a teacher has rubbed my nose in the profound and unaffected admiration of today's students for the pop poets (and their equally unaffected indifference to other poets). It depresses me to have their praises sung at nearly every tutorial and still more to hear the grounds of the praise: that these poets are instantly understandable, warmly human and iconoclastically witty. As an example of the iconoclastic wit I am given Roger McGough's daringly original 'time wounds all heels'. When I mention that Groucho Marx said it first I am considered academic. These students are taking Honours degrees in English, and if ever in preparation for the modern paper they are invited to discuss any major poet of their own choice we are sure to get at least one of the Liverpool poets.

Well, that's how Patricia Beer sees the situation, and a pretty depressing one it is. But how did those Honours students get there in the first place? Not, I'd guess, by enthusing about the wit and wisdom of Roger McGough, but by assiduous parroting of the precept and practice of Richards, Empson, Leavis, Eliot: by playing at school the careful, complex game they were encouraged to play. Filtered down, passed on at umpteenth hand, debased and diluted and sometimes perverted, notions of 'critical reading', of 'the words on the page', of the 'objective correlative', would have been absorbed in countless schoolrooms for purely schoolroom purposes – to make the right gestures in the right context, to pass exams.

And then what? There's something split-minded here, surely. As sixth-formers, these students were being trained in sophisticated techniques which seemed to them to have nothing to do with their own emotional drives and responses. Taught to look for 'complexity', they looked for it, and managed to come back with it: Donne and Hopkins and Auden were laid out and dissected with all the apparatus modern criticism could buy. If it wasn't complex, it wasn't likely to be first-rate. Think of that ominous remark from one of the Pelican Guides to English Literature, first published in 1956 and steadily reprinted ever since. Writing of Herrick, the critic says: ' "Gather ye rosebuds" is a pleasant version of the *carpe diem* theme but it lacks complexity.' Those last four words ought to carry italics, as representative of the kind of thing a student audience has simultaneously swallowed and rejected.

There has been, in fact, a widespread revulsion against such an attitude, and the stance it's taken has been anti-critical and anti-intellectual. It's not easy to document this, since of its very nature the populist movement isn't much interested in writing and publishing critical polemics. But an easily available piece of evidence is the 'Afterwords' written by Michael Horovitz to his Penguin anthology, *Children of Albion*. Here we have an impassioned, exalted testament by someone who went through the Eng Lit mill of school and Oxford, and at the end of it felt that his 'real' psyche had been frustrated, stunted, even conned, by the schoolroom tradition I've talked about:

> At Oxford I saw budding talents buried alive, most elegantly taught to lie, still most persuasively cast in Eliot's calligraphy of dry bones. Legions of professional hollow men – brandishing standards of the New Criticism and *New Lines* – re-laid their trenches, held the muddied field and apportioned the spoils. Their conformist programme, which defined poems as 'the words on the page', proved a two-dimensional concept-cage; a counter too rigid and too myopic for those
>
> to whom the miseries of the world
> Are misery, and will not let them rest
>
> – who seek at the height, with the Shade of Hyperion, to 'think of the earth'. Happily (almost imperceptibly, as far as official recognition is concerned) poetic controls have shifted over these years – to the unlocked word-hoards of poets who *practise* their art. No place for them in the educational system – as it stood then, anyway.

How does this square with what my Cambridge friend said about the impossibility of getting his students to read straightforwardly and simply? It seems to me a matter of context. Given an academic situation, the student will do what he's been trained to do, whether it makes sense to him or not. But he won't bring to the work in hand a wholeness of response or even the full play of his intelligence, because part of him feels that he's inherited a meaningless and arid methodology. The art that really touches him will be spontaneous, easy, unambiguous, untouched by academicism and disapproved of by it.

Anti-intellectual, anti-critical attitudes like these don't lack an ancestry and allegiances. There's the enthusiasm for the sort of forces that Blake is supposed to represent: different but unified aspects of this can be seen in the tone and title of *Children of Albion*, and in Adrian Mitchell's theatrical display, *Tyger*, recently put on at the National Theatre. This enthusiasm for the 'poet-priest' attaches itself to whatever is rhapsodical and seemingly out of control, whether it's Rimbaud as seen by Barry MacSweeney, or a more recent figure such as Allen Ginsberg. But there's a whole mesh of influences and allegiances, some of them, I think, going back to notions of the Romantic Revival, others unacknowledged and perhaps not even recognized, but strikingly similar in tone: I'm thinking of the remarks made from time to time in the pages of *Poetry London* during the Forties – and it may be significant that Tambimuttu evidently has thought the time ripe for a return to England, after over twenty years' absence. In the so-called 'Letters' with which he prefaced a number of the issues of *Poetry London*, Tambimuttu wrote such things as this:

> If criticism has its origin in life, very little adverse criticism on modern poets need be written (if we reserve the term 'poet' for a man who possesses a certain standard of Being and expression). Each poet is a leaf, a significant leaf, of Poetry, the multifoliate tree. The critic is not our concern. Let him get squashed under his own microscope. As Shakespeare did, we will give the public what they want, and to hell with critics! Life is simple, living is simple, the roots of thought are simple. It is only intellectualization that is complex.

All this sounds like an uncanny pre-echo of the open, inclusivist, multi-media, anti-intellectual pronouncements or asides of such present-day figures as Jeff Nuttall, Adrian Henri and Michael Horovitz. Today, it's true, they tend to bandy about such terms as 'Establishment' – a term not invented in the Forties – with which to characterize the enemy. And since they have no lack of access to such supposed pillars of the Establishment as the Arts Council and the BBC itself, their complaints may sound empty or overblown. But that isn't the real or central point.

The real point is that we seem to have reached a state of deadlock or separatism in poetry, with, on one side, a belief in the transparent virtues of spontaneity, immediacy, an energy released by both poet and audience in an instant flash of communion; and, on the other, a conviction that art has a great deal to do with shape, form, control, and that a good poem shouldn't reveal all its facets and depths and resonances at a single hearing or reading. Heaven knows, these aren't new dichotomies, but the camps are clearly enough marked as warring ones in, for example, the statements published in the issue of *the Review* I mentioned. One side seems to see itself in revolt against what it takes as unimaginative, entrenched authority, people whom it sneeringly characterizes as 'self-appointed guardians of the sacred flame'. The other side is deeply contemptuous of (to quote David Harsent) 'those who flash their liberal credentials at the teenybopper market', and (to quote Roy Fuller) of 'the ranks of the illiterate' raising 'their puerile and rhythmless voices'.

It would be possible to demonstrate – or to try to demonstrate – that the so-called Underground attitude to poetry links up with other attitudes to make a whole current nexus of dissidence: dissillusion with parliamentary government, the flexings of student power, the move of the middle-class young along with the working-class away from a literate culture to a primarily oral one, the distrust of the formalized and the structured everywhere, even the whole business of mind-blowing and drugs. But to do so would be both tendentious and repetitious. More interesting to me are the reflections caused by the dream or nightmare with which I began this talk – because they seem to show that even someone like myself, who has little patience with pop poetry and its environs, isn't happy about the critical methodology under which I was brought up and against which the Underground has revolted. Have several generations indeed been crippled in their imaginations by what Horovitz calls 'the professional hollow men, brandishing standards of the New Criticism'? Have the what I would call mindless simplicities applauded by Patricia Beer's students been brought about, and their audience created, directly by a failure of teaching, a dreary rigidity of paraphrase, verbal scrutiny and insistence on the value of complexity? The critic as interpreter of an unfamiliar tongue, as leader through the dangerous minefield of ambiguity and footnote, as demonstrator of a picture which changes and reforms itself at his behest has this man forced things to their apparent state of deadlock?

I don't know. But I found, for example, when I spent last summer on the campus of the University of East Anglia, that many students felt frustrated and choked by their literary syllabus: those of them who had notions, explicit or diffident, of being creative felt no relationship whatever between the kind of work they felt called upon to do as students and their own literary aspirations. Of course, they were naive in many ways; the kind of resentment they felt could be seen, brutally, as a disinclination to work hard; they were often opinionated without having much firm ground of fact on which to base their opinions. All of that can be said about them. I recognize the patronizing air with which I say it, but I could also recognize the dilemma they were in, and could see something of what had caused it. They had been through the mill and had come out as chaff. Years of 'Tradition and the Individual Talent', *Principles of Literary Criticism*, *Seven Types of Ambi-*

guity and *Revaluation* (with all the derivatives and by-products of these) had made them incapable of looking at literature with other than an over-subtlety, an ingenuity, as fatigued as it was detachable. 'Criticism' stank in their nostrils.

But what am I advocating? How is it possible to read simply without just becoming simplistic? Can we do it without becoming childishly retrogressive and adopting an array of crude anti-intellectual dogmas? Certainly I can't be – nobody can be – prescriptive and categorical about the kinds of poem to be written under the New Order. And I'm far from pressing the claims of those large but enfeebling visions of something called 'creativity' in the schools. Perhaps I can quote from my own contribution to the *Review* symposium: 'For every potential poet who is choked in the schoolroom by unimaginative formal teaching ("Write a prose paraphrase in not more than 50 words of 'O Rose thou art sick'.") there must be a dozen who are given false and grandiose notions of a vocation by sloppy encouragement of "creativity". No one should emerge from school with the idea that writing poetry is easy, or that it is primarily "self-expression".' It may seem to be contradicting myself here, but I think not: I'm in fact reinforcing my argument that we're in a state of deadlock, and that soon the camps may be so divided that one side won't be able to communicate with the other – indeed, won't even want to communicate. And this will cause a serious split in our literary culture, with the followers of academic rigour and complexity becoming increasingly more isolated, more Alexandrian in their narrowness and impotence, and the exuberant mind-blowers levelling the whole scene of expectation and performance to something instantaneous, ingratiating, shallow and quickly obsolete. Already the idea that art has something to do with permanence is derided in many quarters, and built-in obsolescence may soon seem to be as relevant to the products of the Muse as it does to the motor-car. Poems by a whole range of latter-day troubadours and itinerant reciters are conceived to be of the moment, for the moment, and indeed in a sense only to exist in an ephemeral relationship with the audience that hears them. The discrediting of, or the ignoring of, the complexities of our inherited and still continuing literary culture by many of the young sometimes makes me wonder whether the over-publicized and cloudy pronouncements of McLuhan, now so little discussed, didn't have at least some gloomily truthful forecasts in them.

A commentator such as A. Alvarez, apparently so disillusioned or unillusioned now that he no longer bothers even to look at what's going on, might dismiss the whole thing – all this talk of 'two camps' and 'deadlock' and so forth – as what he once called 'gang-warfare': something which he saw ten years ago, in his introduction to the Penguin *New Poetry*, as particularly rife on the English literary scene. But I think that trivialises the position. That we're in a divided and quarrelsome state is apparent to anyone who reads the number ot *the Review* from which I've been quoting: but if you disregard the jealousies and pompous proclamations and log-rolling and all such surface dust raised by what can quite legitimately be called 'gang-warfare', you can see a more basic instability. And the fact that some of the best-known poets of one persuasion are absent – I'm thinking, for example, of Adrian Mitchell, Brian Patten, Roger McGough and Michael Horovitz himself – may simply serve to emphasize the split: because such poets would probably think it utterly pointless to take part in such a symposium on what they'd consider unfriendly territory. They have their loyal public, which doesn't give a damn about 'the poetry scene', and that is that.

I said earlier that I can't be prescriptive, and that's

true. This doesn't mean that I'm not bewildered and indeed distressed by what seems to be happening. I don't think that one can just amiably sit back and say: 'Ah well, good poems will go on being written, I expect: time will sort everything out.' I have no doubt that Philip Larkin, say, will continue to write poems that stand above the battle, but what worries me is whether there'll be a public that recognizes their merit.

In an educational set-up torn between syllabus demands of a traditional and too often irrelevant sort and vaguely permissive gestures towards self-expression and undifferentiated creativity, I can see a future coming when there will be two poetries: one the preserve of school-teachers and dons who go on talking in a lecture-room vacuum about form and standards and interpretation, and who manipulate people through exams, and the other a blurred area dominated solely by sensation and fashion, and having the popular and fluent transience of the record charts. You can blame whoever you like – T. S. Eliot or Bob Dylan, the meritocracy or the capitalist proletariat – for the possibility of such a future. But blaming a gulf is an unprofitable business, and even shouting across it is becoming more and more difficult.

The Listener

Roy Fuller **Who Needs a Poetry Reviewer?**

Many poets who have published books over the last ten years have felt themselves imperilled by the existence of Ian Hamilton. It was said, with some justification, that his stringent views were put out not only under his own name in the *London Magazine* and the *Observer* but also under the cloak of anonymity in the *Times Literary Supplement* and in the personae of 'Edward Pygge' and 'Peter Marsh' in the little magazine edited by him, *the Review*. I for one welcomed his appearance on the poetry-reviewing scene, having great sympathy for his principles of literary judgment and (what in a way is of equal importance) the tart and often comic terms in which he disposes of the pretentious and the over-estimated.

The latter business is what is usually more in question. Is there any need to be so devastating? Is there a gratuitous streak of cruelty, even envy or malice, in a critic who expresses himself so waspishly? Are there any Keatses who have been snuffed out by a Hamilton article? I came myself to modern poetry at the time of the founding of *New Verse*, whose editor, Geoffrey Grigson, was no less sharp in his condemnations than Hamilton; and *the Review* undoubtedly took up the torch that Grigson had relinquished over twenty years earlier. Grigson's manner possibly derived most from Wyndham Lewis: behind him, too, was the reputation-deflating side of *The Calendar of Modern Letters*. And farther back was Ezra Pound's struggle against the poeticism of the earlier part of the century.

More remote genealogy would be unprofitable, but of course it can be said that in every epoch poetry is under an obligation to war against the dunces as well as to create its fresh triumphs, and I think that many poets have always felt (possibly, in the last analysis, erroneously) that the latter depended in some way on the former. Some poets, admittedly, have happily got on with the creative process aside from the polemics of their time, but who is to say that they haven't benefited from the dirty in-fighting conducted by those almost agonizingly concerned to promote the good and bash the bad?

Contemporary art is always almost all rubbish. And of the part that isn't rubbish, a substantial proportion is doomed to fairly speedy extinction. But contemporary art has a special meaning for its contemporaries. I talked not long ago to Hallam Tennyson for a radio programme produced by him about his famous ancestor, and listening subsequently to the symposium of views he had assembled I wished I'd made the point that Tennyson is also interesting to us because he is the nearest in time of the line of great established English poets. The rubbish is burnt up by time, yes, but what also goes is the poetic expression of much of our temporal interests. There is a sense in which even a minor poet of today has more to say to us than the illustrious poets of the past.

Because of poetry's slenderer historical thread, the serious poetry reviewer, far more than the fiction reviewer (or probably any other kind of reviewer), is aware of long perspectives and 'eternal' standards. In his judgments of the contemporary he will always have in mind the best of the past. He will be able to discard the obvious tripe (unless it has been so valued elsewhere as to need shredding first) but, even so, much of what he is left with he will try to bury rather than praise. Luckily for the poets involved he will have areas of indulgence, despite his high standards. For one thing, the 'contemporary' interest I have referred to will operate; and in any case no reviewer can take the place of the often over-done depredations of time.

I said 'the serious poetry reviewer'. Perhaps I ought also to have qualified the beast with the epithet 'young'. I don't know how long a critic can continue to treat the books of verse put before him as though they were documents on which society's survival depended. It is not merely a matter of the reviewer mellowing with age (though that is a fairly inevitable process): there must usually come a point where fine discrimination and high principles pass over into eccentricity and crustiness. The serious young poetry reviewer is to some extent a propagandist for his own style and that of his friends, the style that he wants to take over from the styles of the past and prevail over the styles that are currently in competition. When he and his generation have at last gone their separate ways, some perhaps superannuated, what remains, critically speaking, may be mere prejudice, an antiquarian attitude. On the other hand, one must say that an early sharp critical stance may well go with a continuing creativity in maturity and old age. Pound is the great exemplar here, and it's not incongruous to refer to Grigson in the same breath. The latter's critical condemnations have no doubt become too thorough as his poetic pets have died or fallen off – fresh sympathy has been somewhat lacking – but the dissatisfied mind has led to better and better verse of his own. Ian Hamilton (now in his mid-thirties) has scarcely seen the arrival of a new generation with a new style to offer and try to establish, so in his case the test has not yet arisen. It's true that he has admitted younger poets to the exiguous verse pages of *the Review*, but they have usually been writing in a style that he has always allowed or that his critical antennae were anticipating.

Of course, these generalities about a critic's progress depend much on the principles he is applying. Grigson, for instance, I suppose began with the evils anatomized by I. A. Richards very much in mind, sentimentality and over-inflated emotion particularly to be watched. And he would chalk up to a poet's credit his own virtue as a poet with an eye for external appearances. Hamilton's ultimate appeal is to the human, basically Leavisian but without any trappings about anti-human technological civilization, a pre-industrial state of grace, or a mode of salvation. Poetry is to depict the human with all its weakness, irredeemability and messiness; and the failure of Eliot's poetry to do this in a celebratory way is at the core of Hamilton's Eliot criticism. Human joy and suffering, or, at any rate, their poetic delineation, are values in themselves.

Towards the end of its life *New Verse* began to look much more like a left-wing periodical. However, I doubt whether ideology ever played much part in Grigson's judgment of poetry, unless it can be said that in the context of his early times rational intelligibility had political connotations. Hamilton certainly is usually seen to be applying purely literary criteria: even his appeal to the amount of felt life reflected by the poet he makes only in cases, I think, where the poet's undoubted skill and talent require some further explanation of his failure. Even his attack on Robert Lowell's *Notebook* is conducted in literary terms.

As a young man in the 'thirties I wrote a few poetry notices. Had they come early in the epoch I should have felt compelled to do them largely in (elementary) Marxist terms. As it was, I expect they are permeated by a Marxist flavour, irrelevant in general to the business in hand. After the War I engaged in a fair amount of poetry reviewing for *The Listener*, in which my main preoccupation was to try to slaughter the archaic and romantic, then flourishing. Later, in the *London Magazine* under John Lehmann, I did another stint, when, as I recall, I wasn't altogether grateful for the sober poetry of the 'Movement' poets which had come in answer, as it were, to my previous demands. But I'm sure that as a poetry reviewer I improved; and if I were now to take it on regularly again (which God forbid) I think I should be better still. Mainly, I feel I can now discount symptoms which, though obtrusive, are not finally decisive about poetry's endurance. To take an example not intended to be invidious, I believe I could judge a new book by Edmund Blunden more justly than in the past, having come to see the merits in that poet's work aside from the often off-putting diction and sentiments which mark a deal of it.

I don't think this is merely the mellowing process: part of the better perspective stems from increased knowledge and the continuing practice of the poetic art oneself, and part because as a critic I could hardly have got worse. But whether a critic's sympathy can be rightly broadened without an austere past and a continuing testy present seems to me doubtful. Certainly one doesn't want eclecticism in a poetry reviewer; nor kindness, nor a fear of hurting friends, nor any sort of awe that a poet should have laboured to produce a volume. *Per contra*, he should, I believe, have a soft spot somewhere. Undoubtedly it has got to be in the right place – in the brain, absolutely not; and neither quite in the heart or genitals. The case of Geoffrey Grigson and Wallace Stevens is instructive (the business is summarized in my book *Owls and Artificers*). To knock Stevens in 1936, as Grigson did, was legitimate, if somewhat perverse; to speak of his 'non-poetry', having the whole corpus of his work to refer to, seems to me to betray a certain smallness of spirit. Stevens's stature may still be a matter of argument, but that the author of the *Collected Poems* and *Opus Posthumous* is a poet from whatever angle he is viewed is surely indisputable.

Oddly enough, Ian Hamilton's review of the *Letters of Wallace Stevens*, though finally with humorous exasperation acceding to Stevens's life-style, is also deficient in sympathetic appreciation of what, after all, is nearly 900 pages of some of the most distinguished epistolary prose in English. Moreover, there is in the letters, as in the poetry, a concern for the human condition all the more poignant for its oblique expression. It's in relation to this that Hamilton's ultimate appeal to the 'human' betrays itself as inadequate, I think. The merely human, the human without art, without the reference to art's transforming and enhancing powers, the human without all that makes for art, whether it knows it or not – what is this but the merely animal or some essentially ludicrous Lawrentian primitive dream?

However, Hamilton's reviewing rarely comes to this sort of crunch. Its distinguishing method of approach, and one which pays off again and again, is the historical. How illuminating, in a notice about the English appearance of William Carlos Williams's *Pictures from Breughel* in 1964, to be told about Williams's early imagist past; and to be reminded, after John Berryman's emergence as a cult figure, of the side of that poet that made him an orthodox 'thirties writer. Such selective and unobtrusive scholarship has also been a general feature of *the Review*. It may seem an elementary requirement in a reviewer, but it is one which is not often adequately fulfilled.

Is poetry reviewing important? Is the concern for its standards that I've been trying to express here more than the elevation of some minority hobby, like collecting match-boxes? To my mind the answers are all the more unquestionably affirmative in these days when poetry itself is no longer the guardian of the language. More than ever in my lifetime, poetry needs the auxiliaries of good reviewers not merely to rid it of sentimentality and worn-out diction, but also to defend syntax and traditional craft – and even to watch for the muddy dilutions of pornography. (As I write, I see an advertisement in the *New York Review of Books* for a poetry magazine 'to end poetry magazines' – a tape cassette: 'No paper, no type – only the poet's own voice cradling, hurling, caressing, sharing the poems which it uniquely holds.') Also, it seems to me that the academic has become less reliable as an arbiter of poetic taste and judgment. The reviewer has an increasingly important role to play in the longer-term establishment (or demolition) of reputations. One may often ask in vain for the hard-cover critic to rid us of the phoney, or the anthologist to admit the deserving.

Rather in the way that as one grows old one comes to value imaginative skill in a poet, aside from the polemics of the time or of past times, so one warms to intelligent interpretation in a critic, whatever his other qualities or drawbacks. There is usually little question that Ian Hamilton knows what poems mean, a far rarer virtue than may be thought. Not for him the speculative paraphrases particularly beloved by American critics, vacuuming up every scrap of association and knowledge in their own – not necessarily the poet's – minds. Nor is he ever blank before a poetic text: his own scrupulousness as a poetic practitioner gives him an insight which I think few of his genuine victims would want to complain about. The impatience with the emotionally deformed (the unexpressed standards applied here being perhaps an impossible health) time may mitigate: the wit and vigour of expression, the attentive and subtle reading, one hopes will go on.

Encounter

Edwin Brock Keep off the Grass

Christmas brought the kind of coincidence we've all experienced when, discovering a new word, we suddenly see it plastered everywhere. It cropped up first in the British Poetry issue of *Antaeus*. In his introduction to the issue, Douglas Dunn quotes Donald Davie on English poetry: 'an apparent meanness of spirit, a painful modesty of intention, extremely limited objectives' (strange words coming from that source). A couple of days later the postman delivered the December issue of *American Poetry Review* in which Donald Hall speaks of English poetry as 'impeded by a set of silly ideas' the chief of which is modesty.

I had not known modesty had undone so many.

Now the *Antaeus* selection of British poetry is a fair one, by which I mean that it is a fair cross-section of middle-weight poets writing in England today. There is a lot of good poetry in it and no great poetry. And I would expect a similar cross-section of American poetry to reflect just about the same standard . . . modesty or no modesty. So what *is* making Donald Hall's beard bristle? I suspect it is a lack of sympathy with a certain fashion which has prevailed in English poetry for twenty years. Incidentally, Larkin has done as much to encourage this fashion as anyone – Hall can't have his cake *and* eat it.

Hall defines this as 'a schoolboy convention of modesty' a desire 'not to stand out from the crowd' or 'stick your neck out'. This has led, he believes, to an England 'full of poets who play it safe, editors who settle for the modesty of the art they put their lives to, and critics ready to pounce on a sign of ambition, calling it pretentious'.

The thing that puzzles me about this is that I have never met a modest poet (and a modest critic is even more unthinkable). To me, the word Poet is synonomous with Egocentric and I do not see how it can be otherwise. Is it likely that such a creature would fail because of a surfeit of modesty! The question is rhetorical. I don't deny that Donald Hall has a real point (or as real as any sweeping generalization can ever be) but I believe he is so far removed from the English mores, despite his flying visits, that he has got things arse-about-face. The *small*ness he is describing derives not from modesty but snobbery – the vice of a society which is as class-ridden in the 1970s as it was in 1870.

To explain what I mean, I must go back to *Antaeus*. The issue kicks off with a quotation from W. H. Auden, the archetypal mid-Atlantic: 'One demands two things of a poem. Firstly, it must be a well-made verbal object that does honour to the language in which it is written. Secondly, it must say something significant about a reality common to us all, but perceived from a unique perspective. What the poet says has never been said before, but, once he has said it, his readers recognize its validity for themselves'. That is not, to my way of thinking, an ideal definition of a poem but it does highlight the two aspects of poetry which have preoccupied English writing for the past fifty years: 'the well-made verbal object' and 'the unique perspective'. There seems to be something about these two concepts which the English find mutually exclusive, and, under various banners, they have been rallying cries for half a century.

During, and immediately after, the war, the unique-perspectivists were very much in the ascendancy. Calling themselves Neo-romantics, Apocalyptics or latter-day surrealists, they claimed the allegiance, often without the poets' consent, of such as Thomas, Barker, Gascoyne etc. and found their theorist in Herbert Read. Art was therapy. Psychoanalysis and art walked hand in hand. Poetry was such stuff as dreams are made on and you rolled it out of your belly in one long incantatory groan. Of course, this is another sweeping generalization: plenty of good controlled poetry was being written but, at the time, this was seen as harping back to the Thirties; the future was noisier and altogether more exciting.

For about ten years, they dominated magazines such as *Poetry London* and *Poetry Quarterly* and had their fair share of space in the few weeklies which published poetry. But by the early fifties they had run out of steam, or possibly, in the post war austerity years, run out of suitable growing conditions.

In any event, when, in 1956, the well-made-verbal-objectivists, calling themselves The Movement, made their counter-attack in Robert Conquest's *New Lines*, there was practically nothing left to resist. A few overblown reputations were dumped, to be replaced by a few new overblown reputations, and a few editors changed their racing stables. The TLS said, approvingly: 'These new poets are all makers rather than bards . . . All speak in a quiet . . . tone of voice . . . Their poems tend to be reflective rather than directly lyrical . . . arriving at some sort of miniature judgement on life. All of them think of the poem as an instrument for self-criticism rather than for mere self-utterance'. The Pax Romana has lasted well. Since then there have been only minor skirmishes: Movement versus Mavericks, London versus Provinces and something called the Mersey Sound which owed its impact more to a football team and a pop group than any serious literary contribution.

All this would be of no more than archivist interest were it not for one more-or-less permanent after-affect. Whereas the wartime romantics flourished in a non-specialist environment in which ordinary non-academic people read and tried to write poetry. The Movement was a University phenomenon. It insisted that its followers demonstrate their familiarity with the rules of prosody as though before an examiner and, like Living, it left Emotion to its servants. This wasn't modesty, this was an élite closing its ranks to those without its academic training and ambitions. In its own terms, it was being Anti-sloppy. The Movement, as a movement, was short-lived. In 1963 Robert Conquest brought out *New Lines 2* but by this time the demarcation lines had become so blurred that even I was included. The lines have gone on blurring ever since, but old graduates neither die nor fade away, they become the establishment: the establishment in publishing, broadcasting and education; they write the important reviews in the opinion-forming periodicals and they edit the most prestigious anthologies.

It is this academic influence which Donald Hall has called modesty and I have defined as snobbery. And it is this influence which fills English anthologies with poems which are notable only for the complexity of their stanza forms and the erudition of their references. Poems which are, in fact, complex 'Keep off the grass' notices. With the well-made-objectivists so long in the ascendancy, one would have expected, in the nature of things, a series of uprisings from the unique-perspectivists. This has not happened, presumably because no one of sufficient stature has popped up from that side of the fence. In fact, where anti-academic poets have published together as a group, the results have been so non-shattering that they must have confirmed the adherents of the old Movement in their original Anti-sloppy intentions. I say this despite the popularity of the Liverpool group, whose sucess I believe is due to extra-literary factors. Obviously, a piece of mini-journalism like this must leave enormous holes. There are many good poets writing, and publishing, in England, poetry which communicates a unique perspective within a well-made object. But a gap has grown up between the intentions of English poetry and American poetry which does not become smaller as the Atlantic shrinks to a few hours. For convenience, I have labelled this dichotomy IT IS/I AM.

The Englishman, especially the academic Englishman, does not like the first person singular pronoun. It embarrasses him. It signifies either the braggart, the whiner or the exhibitionist, none of whom should, properly speaking, be writing poetry. The use of the word 'I' is permitted where it is used in a self-deprecating manner, where it is so far in the past that it is historical, where the speaker plays such a small part in the material of the poem that he is almost an invisible observer, or where the speaker has assumed an identity which is not that of the poet. In other words, 'I' must be kept in its place: it must be as manipulable as any other part of the poem, and what 'I' sees, feels, thinks or aspires to must be kept under the same close control. Everyone is happier with the Royal 'We', and happier still with the impersonal 'It'. Thus the English critic is more comfortable with descriptive poetry than self-involved poetry, and prefers a crow's eye view of the world to Ted Hughes'. (I say this not to minimize the strength of Hughes' animal poetry, which I admire, but to make the point that he did himself and the critics a favour by assuming a mask, particularly a mask as literary as familiar animals of the English countryside.)

Having, as an editor, had to suffer reams of first person singular outpourings, I have a great deal of sympathy with this attitude, and would not go too far in knocking it. But it does have obvious dangers: I do not believe a poem like *Howl* could have had its first publication in this country; if by some miracle it had, it would, in all probability, have lain unnoticed in some small magazine forever. Lowell is different: his I obeys the rules.

Having said all this, I must say that I believe English poetry today is in perfectly good health from the point of view of what is being *written*. What it sadly lacks is the kind of attention poetry receives in the States. Donald Hall's flying visit does not accord with my own long, grey residence. The amount of money the Arts Council gives to poetry would not keep an American magazine solvent, sales of even relatively established poets seldom creep out of the hundreds, poetry readings are held to audiences of thirty or forty people (in London, not some thatched village), the BBC support poetry to the tune of one half-hour broadcast once a month (radio) and poets only appear on television if they can sing, dance or tell a joke.

Not that there isn't evidence that a bigger audience, partially uncovered by *Penguin Poets*, is out there waiting. It may be that recent American poetry might tempt them, although I do find in post-beat poetry a kind of 'let it all hang out' bravado which, for me, has as many dangers as the over-controlled 'I'. There is, after all, an obverse side to the coin of modesty, and if the too-controlled poem invites the reaction 'So what!', the uncontrolled 'I am' poem invites 'Big deal!'

What always seems to be missing in this kind of Lit. Crit. argument is the fact that the best poetry is existential, i.e. it does not *describe* experience, it *makes* it. The depth and value of the experience must, therefore, play a large part in assessing the poem. And, in all probability, the depth and value of the experience will differ from reader to reader: what one reader finds profound, another will find obvious and superficial (like that statement!). So that the assessment of a poem often becomes little more than a process of head-counting, and the poem's reputation depends upon who wrote what about it where (which brings us back to where we started). All I would add as a PS is a plea for some of us to realize that 'I' is as fictive as any other character in a poem, and must be developed with the same loving care and economy; and for others to realize that Ted Hughes knows at least as much about life as any crow.

Ambit

W. H. Auden

I was one of those who welcomed the young, first Auden, and now after nearly 50 years I sit down, on a cold half-sunny morning, the summer over, to write him a goodbye. No, I was not one of his intimate friends, many times as he befriended me. I knew him on and off, loving him, fearing him a little, as we often fear – and perhaps should fear – the great artists encountered by us on the outside of their inexplicable work. I revered him – 'him' including himself and his writing. I could offer by broad conviction that the English, and the English-speaking, are left now – only for a while, no doubt – without any master of verse, without any master, in any kind of writing, of his wit and penetration and imaginative charity. But I couldn't provide one of those confident surveys and assessments of the Land of Auden.

To be honest, their contemporaries are likely to be poor or only partial guides to the totality, including the middle works, and the late works, of great men. Contemporaries live most in the work they first recognized. I live – perhaps they are the best if not the most profound, depth not being all – in the poems of his earlier books and collections up to *New Year Letter*. I suppose that later on when he thought better, and embraced more—

> How hard it is to set aside
> Terror, concupiscence and pride,
> Learn who and where and how we are,
> The children of a modest star,
> Frail, backward, clinging to the granite,
> Skirts of a sensible old planet

– he no longer composed so well.

Looking backwards, then, I ask how do we first detect – or rather how do we so often miss – the new writer? The first poem I remember by Auden, never republished, and I have never hunted it out again, seems to me to have risen out of an 'Englishness' (he was English, after all) until then unexpressed or not isolated in a poem. Auden was reading English, English at Oxford involved him in Old English, which involved him in *Beowulf*. In the poem he saw the blood-trail which had dripped from Grendel on the way back to his mere, after his arm and shoulder had been ripped off by Beowulf. The blood shone, was phosphorescent on the grass – or so I remember the poem (in the *Cherwell* perhaps?). It was as if Auden, this untidy, untied up, short-sighted pallid person from Christ Church, had given imaginative place and 'reality' to something exploited for the Examination Schools, yet rooted in the English origins.

It was the same with many of his early poems, a measure suggesting fatality; assonances and alliterations coming together to make a new verbal actuality as it might be of rock or quartz; a milieu of the profound Midlands, half aboriginal, half soiled or damaged, half abandoned; the very palpable truth of something, emotions and attitudes, that included both anxieties and satisfactions, at once recognizable and pertinent, autochtonic and not provincial, but before then unrecognized (though intimated a little in Housman, and more in Hardy).

In smart Oxford, and the smart Outside, a fashion then was for the frothy, vicious, and selfish; an aesthetic including snobbery re-exhibited for us recently in the detestable diaries of Evelyn Waugh. The contrast. This is England, this is man: this is Us, this is our sensation. We only are. From Auden I first learnt what the trolls in *Peer Gynt* were up to, and amounted to, when they said 'To myself be enough'; and how skilfully and suavely our trollishness disguises itself – like Auden's devil in *New Year Letter*.

Within a few years *The Orators* and *The Dance of Death* and the first *Poems* – already published poems – were coming to me from Birmingham or from the Malverns, and I was publishing them in *New Verse*. They came on half-sheets of paper, on long sheets of foolscap, in that writing an airborne daddylonglegs might have done with one leg, sometimes in pencil, sometimes smudged and still less easy to decipher. Before they went to the printer they had to be typed, and that was like old-fashioned developing in the darkroom, but more certain, more exciting.

At the far end of the enormous room,
An orchestra is playing to the rich

– there was the poem completing itself, coming out clear on the white page, to be clearer still in the galley, first sight of a new poem joining our literature.

Earth turns over, our side feels the cold . . .

England, beginning to widen into the world, the anxiety of the English individual Wystan Hugh Auden beginning to encompass the anxieties of man.

August for the people and their favourite islands . . .
Dear, though the night is gone . . .

A new poetry, poems to appear again in that wonder book, *Look Stranger!* in 1936.

Picking through a folder, from these *New Verse* days, I found this morning, on the back of a sheet of *New Verse* notepaper a statement excerpted from Auden at this early time!

> When a poet is writing verse, the feeling as it were, excites the words and makes them fall into a definite group, going through definite movements, just as feeling excites the different members of a crowd and makes them act together. Metre is group exciting among words, a series of repeated movements. The weaker the excitement, the less words act together and upon each other.

His feeling was already rising to its greatest power to excite. And the early article in which he wrote that, when he was 25, to explain verse to children (and their parents), he called 'Writing, or the Pattern between People'. Between people – even then. Writers 'would like to be read by everybody and forever. They feel alone, cut off from each other in an indifferent world where they do not live for very long. How can they get in touch again?' The wish for company, the desire to make – these, he said, are the respectable reasons for writing.

He had, when he began, no doubts of his vocation; he accepted his gifts, learning and admitting as well where he was limited or fell short. His Oxford tutor told me once, on a night drive between Reading and Oxford during which we talked the whole way of Auden, a story which might have appalled the Auden of his middle or later understanding. As usual he had interviewed his new undergraduates, and he had asked Auden his stock question, after a while.

> Tutor: 'And what are you going to do, Mr Auden, when you leave the university?'
> Auden: 'I am going to be a poet.'
> Tutor: (since something must be said). 'Well, in – in that case you should find it very useful to have read English.'
> Auden: (after a silence). 'You don't understand, I am going to be a great poet.'

Not all of his writing – but who cares, except the pedant who hates and misunderstands both the arts and the readers he thinks he is serving? – is 'great' or free of dullness. The appalling uniqueness of each great writer includes the different proportions in him of fudge and gold. And what writer, Tolstoy, Hugo, Baudelaire, Melville, Shakespeare, is not a warning against demands for a sustained perfection in literature, as if the great writer's graph ascended steeply and at the worst flattened to a long high level? Zigzags are his condition. And Auden had to write for a living, in our indifferent Anglo-Saxony which gets its poems but expects its poets to live on book-reviewing and the free provisions of stale air.

'I am going to be a great poet' – in that early essay I mentioned, he spoke of the writer as being the soil and the gardener: 'The soil part of him does not know what is going on, the gardener part of him has learnt the routine.' Better to be a bad gardener than bad soil, he went on. His soil proved deep and extensive as the Fens. If sometimes he gardened poorer patches of himself, he was a supremely able, dedicated gardener.

Not all of his poems are kind, but most of them are, and he was – exemplifying the unshiftably true fact that the great writer is always, in the base and inside the total of himself, the good man. A book about Auden (though I cannot bear to read such books) which has just been sent to me from Australia, ends with a note by Rex Warner mentioning Auden's great kindliness and the way he inspired 'great affection in all who know him'. To be kind – not to be cruel – isn't to be evasive, and I see as inseparable from his kindliness Auden's much debated Christianity. It has upset old faithfuls, it repels new readers. For me it demands too much of an 'as if' for intellectual assent; but I see it as wrung from Auden by his long look at the muddle, wickedness, goodness, and necessities of men; wrung from him by desperation about ourselves; not as back-sliding, not as a contradiction, but as an enlargement, accepted or no, of his first, limited Marxist cures for our discontent. Aren't poets, in one form or another, naturally religious men, or nothing? His Christianity may not be what we want, it may disappoint us, it may not be what we suppose is most effective, or most enjoyable; but is it discreditable for a poet to find himself – allowing this to have been Auden's location – outside and beyond poetry in the end?

What Auden doesn't do is opt either from us or from our primary world. I see that is why he turned from rather than against, Hardy. When old, Hardy wrote, in strict continuation, that he had not cared for life, but that since life had cared for him he owed it some loyalty; which must have seemed grudging, and more than half defeated. It was unkindliness – unkindness to a man who has to live; and in this world. The unevasive Auden I revere and love, conceived, like Pasternak, that we are guests of existence, which must be honoured, with delight. If that is one reason why he has been a rhythm and a revolving or shifting fixture in our lives, I shall insist that Auden's Long Mynd and Malverns became the hills of the world. He saw man and the world as Langland saw them from the Malverns.

Our English fortune is to share particularities with him, as Americans share them with Whitman or Russians with Pasternak, or the French with Hugo. He is for everyone, for us he is extra, by language, by keepings, and milieu. In *A Certain World*, which he published two years ago (and which by dedication was my ultimate gift from Auden), I was delighted to encounter so much, so late in him, of our primary world, whether, with everything else, in extracts from Cobbett, a winter and mountain poem by an Irishman of the tenth-century, or a poem on roads by Edward Thomas. Who else would have known, say, about Ivor Gurney making delight of the world, in his distress, out of the Malverns or the Cotswolds –

> Up in the air there beech tangles wildly in the wind.

If we follow him round, as he celebrates, investigates, discards, adds, reattempts, we find in him, I declare, explicit recipes for being human. And implicit ones, in poems, stanzas, lines, again and again, which gave us in sound and movement the additional bonus of what their language cannot say. The bonus of great poetry.

Times Literary Supplement

Poems from Magazines

Luna

Where is there an end to it the river of women,
Walking proudly through time on their high heeled shoes,
On their shoulders for a space the weight of being human,
The tale of their being here will never close.

They step into their births and put on sorrow
Like a purple vest, a mantle of dark green,
Then the bow is drawn, the string shoots forth the arrow
And they follow its course to a target that cannot be seen.

The sound of the music of their movement
Sweetens with praise the dull hammer blows of time,
Through the intricate metres of their slow advancement,
God, through his daughters here, is taking aim.

And it unfolds the steel petals of the rose of their being
And scented like the rose in an expanding tense,
They walk with light feet over the apotheosis of ruin
Obeying the far gone conductor of the intolerable dance.

Where is there an end to it, the river of women
Walking proudly in their dust through devious ways
The high keen merriment of the passing
All that is not dust must continually praise.

Outposts

Alan Bold **Widow**

I see a widow standing
Stark in the winter street.
The wind has whipped
Her hair across her chin.
    She is like a bearded lady
In a sideshow.
Yet the black hat, the black
Diamond on the coatsleeve
Are also out of place:
Only
Objects of admiration
Praised by the eyes
Of those who saunter by.
    She should be dressed in white
Like a bride.
She should carry flowers:
Red, yellow, purple.
    Yet
She stands broken like
A snapped twig
Black against the winter sky
And the icy streets.
    A black streetcat nuzzles
Against her best shoes
And she reacts.
    Her life has become hollow
The way a ship does
When it sinks below
The ocean
And cadavers rise to the surface
Like bloated balloons.

Her shoes are weighted
Like diving boots
As she turns from the cat
And walks back through a sea
Of sympathetic faces
She
Will never see again.

Aquarius

Alan Brownjohn **Sporting Event**

Wimbledon. Centre Court. Blank and pitiless sun.
  Many
Eyes misted with, as it were, emotion.

The 'Old Fox' is playing young Kenny Trabner of
  Australia.
The Old Fox sticks to a baseline game, Trabner is
Up at the net for the volleys, leaning back
At unthinkable angles for the smashes. Cunning,
And age, and experience, facing
All the burnished arrogance of youth, Trabner
Playing the ruthless tennis they play now,
And things not going too well at all for the Old Fox.

Trabner, too, in immaculate shorts and crew-cut,
The Old Fox in full-length, pre-war flannels, bald,
And wearing a green eye-shade on his forehead
  above his bifocals;
But the crowd is on his side.

Can the Old Fox do it this time, *can* the Old Fox do it
  again?
Things don't look too well. First set
To Trabner, 6–0. Second set
To Trabner, 6–0. It is crafty tactic the Old Fox is
  trying.
Third set, Trabner leading 5–0 and 40–0 in the sixth
  game,
On his own service.

This will need all the Old Fox can pull out, but
Throughout his career the Old Fox has somehow
  been
Strangely able to pull something out,
So to speak, in moments of crisis.

Now the crowd is utterly still, now the princess
Fingers the Cup, in the Royal Box, with excitement
that mounts weirdly. Trabner
Is serving for the match, three balls bunched
In one broad hand, and
The first ball lifts. And as
The thunderous, upward, apparently final trajectory
Of Trabner's racquet begins, the Old Fox
Pulls out from the pocket of his flannel trousers
An ancient matchlock pistol such as might be hired
For commercial TV serials about the Jacobite
Rebellion,
And fires.
Trabner falls. The crowd is on ten thousand
delirious,
Cheering, swooning feet. With a last
Expenditure of feeling the princess accidentally
shudders the Cup from its plinth.
The Old Fox leaps the net and shakes Trabner's
dying hand.
The newsmen, as they are said to do, crowd round.
The umpire calls out, 'Game, Set, Match and
Championship to the OLD FOX.'

Max Robertson says, 'Yes, the Old Fox has done it
again!'

Encounter

Alan Brownjohn **Letter to America**

I take a long lick of this envelope,
Getting an unsweet, unAmerican taste:
The glue of England, which does not pretend.

The middle-classes drink precisely
From the far side of the other person's cup,
But kiss more deeply than the workers do

– Say sociologists. One day, we parked outside
A backstreet house in Wandsworth, kissing
In just that way, not thinking of social class,

And this in broad daylight, very visibly,
When an aproned lady came out quite displeased,
And motioned to us, literally shaking

Her hand with her wrist as if her hand
Were shaking a duster, wanting us to move on.
The moral disapproval was very clear.

– And the point is, do you remember this at all,
Which came to me as I began to lick
Your envelope? Since, if you don't recall,

Invisible dust, from a hand shaking it, may
Have settled on us and on the Atlantic
Covering anything this letter means.

And need I have unsealed it to say all this?

Outposts

Michael Burn **Growing Up**

When I was very young,
Before war came,
In the wake of someone important
I managed to enter the concentration camp
Of Dachau.

To the important person
The Commandant showed politeness,
And also the inmates.
He might have been showing a hospital
For, mostly, professors and artists.
Except they wore convict clothes;
They looked ill in a different way;
They tried to make signs.
'Don't believe,' they were trying to say.

At the end he asked,
'Can I show you anything else?'
And I asked what was behind
A row of doors.
When they opened one, out fell a man.
Like a plank.
They pushed him back and shut it.
'Some people' explained the Commandant,
'Have to have special treatment.'

That was in Hitler's day.
After the war, under Rakosi,
I had to report a trial.
The accused had been tortured for weeks,
Rehearsed in their confessions,
Then fattened up for the show.
When I got home I was sick.

The night after Dachau
I went to the opera.
The night after the trial
I went to a party.

I've been to other operas,
And to other parties.
About similar trials,
And other places like Dachau,
I have only read since then.

Though I still write about roses and love,
Beautiful people and country,
It would be difficult now to look at the Parthenon
For long, or to walk in a garden,
Without having a vision of somebody falling
And hurriedly slammed back
Between the amber columns,
Or of a line of drugged men
At attention between the flowers.

Encounter

Jim Burns **The Old Revolutionary Speaks**

We began with demands for freedom,
and finished by filling in forms.
After all, what else was there to do?
The bourgeoisie had all been shot,
or at least the three of them
willing to admit to being of that class.
Everyone else wore mufflers and caps,
a little new, perhaps, not frayed
at the edges, but still mufflers and caps,
and none of us wanted to make the mistake
of eliminating a genuine worker.
And the army had been properly purged,
forty captains made corporals,
and forty corporals made captains.
We thus dealt with privilege
by turning things upside down.
We levelled all the hills,
and filled in the hollows, so that no-one
live higher or lower than anyone else,
and we abolished every differential
of money and creed and culture.
All one had to do to obtain one's rights
was fill in a form, and present it
at the right place, at the right time,
and, of course, in the right way.
After all, what else was there to do?
It is only by filling in forms
that one deals with demands for freedom.

Meridian

Stewart Conn **Arrivals**

i

The plane meets
Its reflection on the wet
Runway, then crosses
To where I wait
Behind plate glass.

I watch
With a mixture
Of longing and despair
As you re-enter
The real world.

All we have is each other.
I sometimes wonder
If that is enough;
Whether being together
Enlarges or diminishes grief.

ii

Remember arriving
From Thorame –
The scent
Of honey,
Of lavender clinging.

On the Jonte,
Climbing goat-tracks
To drink from a spring
Under an arch
Of red sandstone.

Or last year,
After a second honeymoon
In Amsterdam, having
Exchanged gifts: a miniature
War-horse, a silver ring.

iii

Tonight your return
From Ulster
Renders
My fears
Unfounded. Yet neither

Of us speaks. Instead
We think of those
Living there, others
Who have died.
Your brother-in-law

Has decided to emigrate:
The one sure escape.
As I draw up
At the lights, you droop
Forward, hands on your lap.

iv

The pubs are coming out.
In Dumbarton Rd
Two drunks, having battered
each other senseless, sit
In their own vomit.

No-one interferes.
It is not easy
To accept that there may
Be a certain mercy
In living here.

The lights turn
To green. I imagine
You lying alone
In a white room, surrounded
By flimsy screens . . .

Scottish International

Douglas Dunn **The House Next Door**

Old dears gardening in fur coats
And 'Hush Puppies', though it's a mild July,
Once met Freddie Lonsdale at John o' Groats.
Their keyboard's Chopin and their humour's wry.
    There's no one I'd rather be called 'famous' by.
    They have an antique goldfish, a cat called Sly.

They live in my unpublished play
For two sad characters. Their Chippendale
Haunts England's salesrooms, their silver tray
That brought Victoria's breakfast and her mail.
    I visit their house. – The coffee's aroma,
    The cat out cold in its afternoon coma!

I watch them watching for the post,
Wondering who writes. In *my* play, no one writes,
They are alone, together, and have lost
Our century by being old. Their nights
    Are spent rehearsing through Irving Berlin;
    The gardens turn to stage-sets when they begin.

My best times with them are 'Chopin
Mornings'; they smile vainly at my small applause –
No one plays the Pole as badly as they can –
And Sly stands up, and purs, stretching his claws,
    Playing his cat's piano on the cushions,
    And called by pianist sisters, Perfect Nuisance.

There garage is pronounced gar*age*,
Strawberries never known as strawbs, but *fraises*,
And cheddar is called cheese, the rest *fromage*,
And all life is a lonely Polonaise.
    Why do I love them, that milieu not mine,
    The youngest, laughingly, 'last of the line'?

No answers. They have given me
Too much for answering. I am their pet,
Like Sly. They have defied me, cutting free
From my invention. 'Let us live. Forget
	You made us up for money. We'll give you tea,
And you shall drive our ancient crock down to the sea.'

Poetry Book Society Christmas Supplement

D. J. Enright

Henri Rousseau's 'Tropical Storm with Tiger', or Home and Colonial

I'm not one of those simpletons who believe
That if only they had a larger TV screen
They would be able to see the naughty bits.
But if that picture were a few inches longer –
Here, on the right-hand side, I mean – then
In fact you would see – not a naughty bit –
You would see me.

Sexual behaviour does exist in the tropics –
Oh indeed – but it's relatively invisible.
It doesn't go on in public. And it wouldn't
Even if there weren't a storm, even if
The jungle weren't so full of spiky things.

Public sex is less sex than public, I reckon.
Like that young couple in the Underground
The other night. They weren't doing anything,
They were simulating it. In my day
We used to dissimulate. And likewise I doubt
This notion that a wider screen induces
A broader mind. What you can see is never
The interesting part. Though of course
I'm not referring to a gentleman like you
Looking at a picture like this
In a reputable gallery.

Imagination is allowed some latitude,
I know (though, as it happens, this painting
Doesn't get enough), but all the same . . .
The jungle's not half as pretty as it looks here,
Untidy at the best, storm or no storm.
The bougainvilia was tatty and blotched,
Not just out of a hot-house. It was gloomy –
That's another thing about jungles – and
The lightning had that lost air it always has

In those parts. Fumbling around for something
To get a grip on, like a roof, a chimney
Or a golf club.

But the tiger – Frenchy's hit it off to a T!
Scared stiff, what with its tail behind, which it
Took for a flying snake, and in front – a hairy
Red-faced white man in a Post-Impressionist sarong,
Heading for the nearest *kedai*.
I fancied an ice-cold Guinness. A moment later
And there'd have been just me on that canvas,
Dry and wet at once, sarong slipping a bit,
Tiger a mile away and still running.

Even so, would you really see more on a larger
 screen,
D'you think? Or do the girls wear towels or
 something?

The Listener

Gavin Ewart Incident Second World War

In Memoriam P. M. B. Matson

It was near the beginning of that war. 1940 or 41,
when everything was fairly new to almost everyone.
The bombing of cities we understood, and blackouts; and certainly, thanks
to the German Army and Air Force, we'd seen dive-bombers and tanks.
But when the fighters came in to strafe with hedge-hopping low attacks
how many bits and pieces would be picked up to fill the sacks?
Aircraft cannon were not much fun for the weary grounded troops
and there wasn't much entertainment when the Stukas were looping loops
but nobody knew *for certain* the percentage who wouldn't get up,
how many would be donating their arms or their legs to Krupp.
So somebody in an office had the very bright idea,
why not set up an Exercise: machine-gunning from the air?
The War Office would know exactly the kind of figures involved,
an exciting statistical problem could be regarded as solved.

In a field, they put khaki dummies, on the reverse side of a hill.
And afterwards, they reckoned, they could estimate the kill.
Opposite these was the audience, to watch the total effect,

a sort of firework display – but free – the RAF being the architect.
All arms were represented? I think so. A grandstand seat
was reserved for top brass and others, a healthy open air treat;
enclosed, beyond the dummies, they stood (or sat?) and smoked
or otherwise passed the time of day, relaxed as they talked and joked.

An experienced Spitfire pilot was briefed to fly over low
and give those dummies all he'd got – the star turn of the show,
with all the verisimilitude of a surprise attack.
Then to his fighter station he would whizz round and back.
They waited. And suddenly, waiting, they saw that angel of death
come at them over the hillside. Before they could draw breath
he passed with all guns firing; some fell on their faces, flat,
but the benefit was minimal that anyone had from that.
He reckoned that *they* were the dummies, in his slap-happy lone-wolf way,
that trigger-crazy pilot. He might have been right, some say.
But bitterness and flippancy don't compensate for men's lives
and official notifications posted to mothers and wives.

Nevertheless, there *were* results; percentages were worked out,
how 10 per cent could be written off, the wounded would be about

50 per cent or so. Oh yes, they got their figures all
right.
Circulated to units. So at least that ill-omened flight
was a part of the Allied war effort, and on the credit
side –
except for those poor buggers who just stood there
and died.

Gavin Ewart **If**

If I ever came back (if we are speaking of
impossibilities
and revenants and scholar gipsies
and belief in time travel and supernatural facilities),
if by some sort of spiritual ellipsis
my entire life could be compressed into one episode
current between the anode and the cathode,

I would choose you to come back to – not in the
inanities
of a daily life spent as a reviewer,
but in a centre of learning, a place where the
humanities
are taught, though few and daily fewer
those who would remember me in its venerable
streets,
while dons lecture on the language of Keats,

and I would meet you in a pub with a garden and
the academic background wouldn't matter
or the centuries in which undergraduate and
ordinand
in rough-walled quads trod the flat stones flatter,
and for one hour we would talk, touch and look –
by heart, not according to the book.

That pub still stands, where I celebrated my affinity
with you; and its trade doesn't slacken;
and the long line of lovers stretches to infinity
in the bed-sitting-room and in the bracken,
and in that walled courtyard with its trees
you and I are the ghostly absentees.

Thom Gunn

Iron Landscape
(and the Statue of Liberty)

No trellises, no vines
                                        a fire-escape
Repeats a bare black Z from tier to tier.
Hard flower, tin scroll embellish this landscape.
Between iron columns I walk towards the pier.

And stand a long time at the end of it
Gazing at iron on the New Jersey side.
A girdered ferry-building opposite,
Displaying the name LACKAWANNA, seems to ride

The turbulent brown-grey waters that intervene:
Cool seething incompletion that I love.
The zigzags come and go, sheen tracking sheen;
And water wrestles with the air above.

But I'm at peace with the iron landscape too,
Hard because buildings must be hard to last
– Block, cylinder, cube, built with their angles true,
A dream of righteous permanence, from the past.

In Nixon's era, decades after the ferry,
The copper embodiment of the pieties
Seems hard, but hard like a revolutionary
With indignation, constant as she is.

From here you can glimpse her downstream, her far
   charm,
Liberty, tiny woman in the mist
– You cannot see the torch – raising her arm
Lorn, bold, as if saluting with her fist.

Barrow Street Pier,
New York

The Listener

Donald Hall **To a Waterfowl**

Women with hats like the rear ends of pink ducks
applauded you, my poems.
These are the women whose husbands I meet cn airplanes,
who close their briefcases and ask, 'What are *you* in?'
I look in their eyes, I tell them I am in poetry,

and their eyes fill with anxiety, and with little tears.
'Oh, yeah?' they say, developing an interest in clouds.
'My wife, she likes that sort of thing? Hah-hah?
I guess maybe I'd better watch my grammar, huh?'
I leave them in airports, watching their grammar,

and take a limousine to the Women's Goodness Club
where I drink Harvey's Bristol Cream with their wives,
and eat chicken salad with capers, with little tomato wedges,
and I read them 'The Erotic Crocodile', and 'Eating You'.
Ah, when I have concluded the disbursement of sonorities,

crooning, 'High on thy thigh I cry, Hi!' – and so forth –
they spank their wide hands, they smile like Jell-O,
and they say, 'Hah-hah? My goodness, Mr. Hall,
but you certainly do have an imagination, huh?'
'Thank you, indeed,' I say; 'it brings in the bacon.'

But now, my poems, now I have returned to the motel,
returned to *l'eternel retour* of the Holiday Inn,

naked, lying on the bed, watching *Godzilla Sucks*
  Mt. Fuji,
addressing my poems, feeling superior, and drinking
  bourbon
from a flask disguised to look like a transistor radio.

Ah, my poems, it is true,
that with the deepest gratitude and most serene
  pleasure,
and with hints that I am a sexual Thomas Alva
  Edison,
and not without collecting an exorbitant fee,
I have accepted the approbation of feathers.

And what about you? You, laughing? You, in the
  bluejeans,
laughing at your mother who wears hats, and at your
  father
who rides airplanes with a briefcase watching his
  grammar?
Will you ever be old and dumb, like your creepy
  parents?
Not you, not you, not you, not you, not you, not you.

American Poetry Review

Tony Harrison **Allotments**

Choked, reverted *Dig for Victory* plots
Helped put more bastards into Waif Home cots
Than anywhere, but long before my teens
The Veterans got them for their bowling greens.
In Leeds it was never *Who* or *When* but *Where*.
The bridges of the slimy River Aire,
Where Jabez Tunnicliffe, for love of God,
Founded the *Band of Hope* in eighteen odd,
The cold canal that ran to Liverpool,
Made hot trickles in the knickers cool
As soon as flow. The graveyards of Leeds 2
Were hardly love-nests but they had to do –
Through clammy mackintosh and winter vest
And rumpled jumper for a touch of breast.
Stroked nylon crackled over groin and bum
Like granny's wireless stuck on Hilversum.
And after love we'd find some epitaph
Embossed backwards on your arse and laugh.
And young, we cuddled by the abattoir,
Faffing with fastenings, never getting far.
Through sooty shutters the odd glimpsed spark
From hooves on concrete stalls scratched at the dark
And glittered in green eyes. Cowclap smacked
Onto the pavings where the beasts were packed.
And offal furnaces with clouds of stench
Choked other couples off the lychgate bench.

The Pole who caught us at it once had smelt
Far worse at Auschwitz and at Buchenwald,
He said, and, pointing to the chimneys, *Meat!*
Zat is vere zey murder vat you eat.
And jogging beside us, *As Man devours*
Ze flesh of animals, so vorms devour ours.
It's like your anthem, Ilkla Moor Baht'at.

Nearly midnight and that gabbling, foreign nut
Had stalled my coming, spoilt my appetite
For supper, and gave me a sleepless night
In which I rolled frustrated and I smelt
Lust on myself, then smoke, and then I felt
Street bonfires blazing for the end of of war
V.E. and J. burn us like lights, but saw
Lush prairies for a tumble, wide corrals,
A Loiner's Elysium, and I cried
For the family still pent up in my balls,
For my corned beef sandwich, and for genocide.

Antaeus

John Hewitt **The King's Horses**

After fifty years, nearly, I remember,
living then, in a quiet leafy suburb,
wakening in the darkness, made aware
of a continuous irregular noise,
and groping to the side-window to discover
the shadow-shapes which made that muffled patter,
passing across the end of our avenue,
the street lamps and the black trees shuttering
a straggle of flowing shadows, endless, of horses.

Gypsies they could have been, or tinkers maybe,
mustering to some hosting of their clans,
or dealers heading their charges to the docks,
timed to miss light's traffic and alarms:
a migration the newspapers had not foretold:
some battle's ragged finish, dream-repeated;
the last of an age retreating, withdrawing,
leaving the kingdom beggared, bereft
of the proud nodding muzzles, the nervous bodies;
gone from us the dark men with their ancient skills
of saddle and stirrup, of bridle and breeding.
It was an end, I was sure; an end of what
I never could tell. It never was reported;
but the echoing hooves persisted. Years after,
in a London hotel in the grey dawn,
a responsible man concerned with certain duties,
I heard the metal clatter of hooves staccato,
and hurriedly leapt to catch a glimpse of my horses,
but the pace and the beat were utterly different:
I saw, by the men astride, these were the King's
    Horses
going about the King's business, never mine.

The Irish Press

David Holbrook

Nearly caught in Bed by the Queen Mum

Clipping yew hedges, the worst job in the garden,
Stripped to the waist, sweating in the hot sun,
Leaf scales sticking to me like ticks,
Dust fouling my eyes and nostrils.
The twigs scratched at my skin, like your fingers
Searching my naked belly, aroused me, and the glad
Dry wreathes of roses everywhere, this year,
Unspoiled good colours, tender in the sun, some
perfect.
Weary, I came in to bath, and stripped beside you.
So, without speaking, we both weighed our chances:
Realizing everyone was out, I feigned
A need for help, and you came innocent,
Or not so innocent, and then protested.

So, you gazed out of the window, doubtful,
Until your body told you what to do: no,
I'll not tell all, about that hour –
You elegant in earrings, me dressed only in scratches,
And how you were so wild you raced me home,
And how, gasping, we laughed, all the way through!

Oh, help! Here comes the Clerk to the Parish
Council:
I dive into my clothes – 'just changing after
gardening'.
Surprise! A Royal Personage visiting the village!
Supposing they had brought Her Majesty round
here?

Ah, well – render unto Caesar the things that are
Caesar's!
Holding one breast and the curved small of your
back
I was a soul in bliss: worshipping the majesty of your
body

I would have had to say: here, Madam, like the
angels,
I am lost in perpetual contemplation of an infinite
glory,
If only for an hour . . .

Critical Quarterly

Richard Murphy **The Reading Lesson**

Fourteen years old, learning the alphabet,
He finds letters harder to catch than hares
Without a greyhound. Can't I give him a dog
To track them down, or put them in a cage?
He's caught in a trap, until I let him go,
Pinioned by 'Don't you want to learn to read?'
'I'll be the same man whatever I do.'

He looks at a page as a mule balks at a gap
From which a goat may hobble out and bleat.
His eyes jink from a sentence like flushed snipe
Escaping shot. A sharp word, and he'll mooch
Back to his piebald mare and bantam cock.
Our purpose is as tricky to retrieve
As mercury from a smashed thermometer.

'I'll not read any more.' Should I give up?
His hands, long-fingered as a Celtic scribe's,
Will grow callous, gathering sticks or scrap;
Exploring pockets of the horny drunk
Loiterers at the fairs, giving them lice.
A neighbour chuckles. 'You can never tame
The wild-duck: when his wings grow, he'll fly off.'

If books resembled roads, he'd quickly read:
But they're small farms to him, fenced by the page,
Ploughed into lines, with letters drilled like oats:
A field of tasks he'll always be outside.
If words were bank-notes, he would filch a wad;
If they were pheasants, they'd be in his pot
For breakfast, or if wrens he'd make them king.

London Magazine

Richard Murphy

Seals at High Island

for Emily

The calamity of seals begins with jaws.
Born in caverns that reverberate
With endless malice of the sea's tongue
Clacking on shingle, they learn to bark back
In fear and sadness and celebration.
The ocean's mouth opens forty feet wide
And closes on a morsel of their rock.

Swayed by the thrust and backfall of the tide,
A dappled grey bull and a brindled cow
Copulate in the green water of a cove.
I watch from a cliff-top, trying not to move.
Sometimes they sink and merge into black shoals;
Then rise for air, his muzzle on her neck,
Their winged feet intertwined as a fish tail.

She opens her fierce mouth like a scarlet flower
Full of white seeds; she holds it open long
At the sunburst in the music of their loving;
And cries a little. But I must remember
How far their feelings are from mine marooned.
If there are tears at this holy ceremony
Theirs are caused by brine and mine by breeze.

When the great bull withdraws his rod, it glows
Like a carnelian candle set in jade.
The cow ripples ashore to feed her calf;
While an old rival, eyeing the deed with hate,
Swims to attack the tired triumphant god.
They rear their heads above the boiling surf,
Their terrible jaws open, jetting blood.

At nightfall they haul out, and mourn the drowned,
Playing to the sea sadly their last quartet,
An improvised requiem that ravishes
Reason, while ripping scale up like a net:
Brings pity trembling down the rocky spine
Of headlands, till the bitter ocean's tongue
Swells in their cove, and smothers their sweet song.

London Magazine

Philip Pacey **Moon**

Stopped here to stare –
at the strangeness of the first star
stuttering over Saunton Down
as a windblown lantern, or
like fire in sunlight, struggling
to outshine a still luminous sky –

you turned, cried, Look at the moon!
and above the dark hill this round
of haloed brimstone, risen behind
our walking soundlessly, as an owl flies.

Critical Quarterly

Peter Reading

Plague Graves

We knew nothing of their existence before
you showed us the other day five wrinkled
knobbly old and enormous fingers
tied down with heather roots tight to the moor;
and they, being buried three hundred years
ago, knew nothing about us, but neither
party's existence was any way less
for the other's ignorance of it.

To see
the same future waiting and still to continue
seems our most noble attribute, though
I suppose we secretly hope for some permanent
monument left of us, some recognition
by those coming after. No chance. Sheep maul
beyond recognition alarmingly quickly
the sandwich-paper memorials left
by charabanc trippers, dissolving all tangible
trace of us.

When the world ends and space-age
picnickers freeze to flint or melt or
asphyxiate or simply, no longer able
to read the already eroding incision,
just think five slabs have rather aesthetically
fallen above Gorse Hill, the result will
undoubtedly be the same in the final
analysis – no one to know them, extol them
or give them permanence in the now prevalent
sense of fame; and their mark will be not
in palpable stone but that they were once,
walked here, and did wonderful things.

Encounter

Jeremy Robson **No Telling Why**

There was no telling why: why
that office, why five twenty nine
that winter's night, files shut,
dull eyes glued to the dawdling clock.
But come it did, and come to stay
it had: there was no coaxing it
from the long shelves, to the rain
arrowing through the kerbside trees.

Its wings were tipped with white
its left leg ringed – not a phoenix
committing its ashes to the desert
wind, rising anew, but a pigeon,
prisoner in an earth-bound room.

Now a Nelson, gazing seaward, his
mind elsewhere, might turn a blind eye
to the birds, vying for peanuts at his
column's foot, spattering his square,
but not we that ringed intruder.

Frightened for it, by it, clumsily
with umbrellas, rulers, chairs
we stalked it, windows wide, sills
laced with bits of biscuit, bread.
Panicked, mistaking our intent,
it shot from side to side, rising
in plane bursts, making us dive.

It went of course at last,
leaving us dazed, in disarray,
each waiting the other's move,
none knowing quite why, having strayed
this way into our ordinary room, it
had wished to stay, why the room
itself had changed, why the city
night was spent now, blank, estranged.

Poetry Book Society Christmas Supplement

Vernon Scannell **Spot Check at Fifty**

I sit on a hard bench in the park;
The spendthrift sun throws down its gold
The wind is strong but not too cold;
Daffodils shimmy, jerk and peck.

Two dogs like paper-bags are blown
Fast and tumbling across the green;
Far off laborious lorries groan.
I am not lonely, though alone.

I feel quite well. A spot-check on
The body-work and chassis finds
There's not much wrong. No one minds
At fifty going the speed one can.

No gouty twinge in toe; all limbs
Obedient to such mild demands
I make. A hunger-pang reminds
I can indulge most gastric whims.

Ears savour sounds. My eyes can still
Relish this sky and that girl's legs;
My hound of love sits up and begs
For titbits time has failed to stale.

Fifty scored and still I'm in.
I raise my cap to dumb applause,
But as I wave I see, appalled,
The new fast bowler's wicked grin.

New Statesman

Michael Schmidt **Litter**

Like eggs impatiently deserted
the owl pellets litter a rough nest –
perfect ovals pressed into the straw
by a heaviness of birds, as bulbs might be
set out in moss this time of year to wait.

The owls gave up the season
and emigrated, leaving their movables,
their straw and spoor, for the fortunate
next-comer. We climb to the high
hollow in the tree.

We look in.
There is down here,
and crook twigs like talons. And the owl
pellets, hard to the touch, scentless,
smooth as shells. A prick with a pen-knife

breaks the first globe, spilling
dust and a clutch of white we blow on
until it is the perfect skeleton
of a mouse curled up, clean as though
a natural death had washed it in the ground.

Another pellet gives up four small teeth
and the whole foot of a bird
unaltered by digestion, splayed as though
standing on firm ground. So it coursed
the body of its predator and did

no damage; and the mouse seems
to have slept its progress through,
intact as bone. What did it have to fear
once the talons ringed and lifted it –
a still, warm burden – home,

certain of the pilot and the port?
The beak that finally had it,
was another burrow merely.
Featherlike it drifted to the pool
of acid and was drowned.

We have no use for it.
It clings to your knife,
a stiff twist of white hair,
a whisker – delicate
child of the night-hunter, inanimate as pearl.

The Listener

James Simmons **The Younger Son**

Natural strength and will
he had, to struggle through thorns
and all to find her room
in one continuous
ambitious movement.
And then he stopped.
Oh, she was beautiful
and so much more than just
asleep, so primly propped.

His body stopped. His mind
ran on to its reward.
From distant times, from fame
and mystery, her hundred
years of sleep, this girl
would rise into his arms.
Down the great stair
they would descend to marriage.
It was his life she would share.

His life? It had been stumbling
in her direction. And what
was she but beautiful?
Yearning for beauty had been
his youthful nature, his dream;
but now, to kiss, to create
a life and offer years
of variable bliss,
what people do in marriage?
The boy was kneeling in tears.

He found himself at a window
rubbing a hole in the dust
to look down on his world
where trees were vaguely waving
with modest signs of spring,
a bloom on the brown branches.

The pane was suddenly wet
with rain. Love was a smile
reflected on his face,
'I'm not dead yet'.

Just walk back to the inn
for peace and comfort, a meal
and a bit of crack with the maid,
and sup mulled wine
maybe, and read by the fire.
He could certainly do with a bath.
Below were the broken branches
and trampled grass that faintly
marked his heroic path.

Right then, a last look,
a tender touch, and goodbye . . .
but horribly he felt
his head bending, his lips
pursing to kiss. On contact
her body writhed with pain,
her eyes were open, her mouth
screaming, himself trapped
in a room trying to explain.

The Honest Ulsterman

Charles Tomlinson **Gladstone Street**

It was the place to go in nineteen-thirty,
And so we went. A housemaid or two
Still lingered on at the bigger houses.
A miner and his family were the next
To follow us there, had scarcely settled in
When the wife began dying, whitely visible
Through the bay window in their double bed.
At the back, the garden vanished
Under grass and a ramshackle shed.
People were sure the street was going downhill.
It literally was: cracks in our hall
Opened as the house started to subside
Towards the mines beneath. Miners were everywhere
Under that cancerous hill. My mother swore
That you could hear them tapping away below
Of a quiet night. Miners unnerved her so
Ever since one sat beside her on the train
And soiled her with his pit dirt. But it wasn't miners
Undid the street. The housemaids lasted
Until the war, then fed the factories.
Flat-dwellers came and went, in the divided houses,
Mothers unwedded who couldn't pay their rent.
A race of gardeners died, and a generation
Hacked down the walls to park their cars
Where the flowers once were. It was there it showed.
The feeble-minded style of the neighbourhood
Gone gaudily mad in painted corrugations,
Botches of sad carpentry. The street front has
  scarcely changed.
No one has recorded the place.
Perhaps we shall become sociology. We have
  outpaced
Gladstone's century. We might have been novels.

London Magazine

Charles Tomlinson **Night Ride**

The lamps are on: terrestrial galaxies,
    Fixed stars and moving. How many lights,
How many lives there are, cramped in beside
    This swathe of roadway. And its sodium circuits
Have ousted the glimmer of a thousand hearths
    To the margins of estates whose windows
Blaze over pastoral parentheses. Scatterings
    Trace out the contours of heights unseen,
Drip pendants across their slopes.
    Too many of us are edging behind each other
With dipped beams down the shining wet.
    Our lights seem more beautiful than our lives
In the pulse and grip of this city with neither
    Time nor space in which to define
Itself, its style, as each one feels
    His way among the catseyes and glittering
        asterisks
And home on home reverberates our wheels.

Poetry Nation

Charles Tomlinson **The Last of Night**

Mist after frost. The woodlands
stretch vague in it, but catch
the rising light on reefs
of foliage above the greyish
'sea' I was about to say,
but sun so rapidly advances
between glance and word,
under that leafy headland
mist lies a sea no more:
a gauze visibly fading
burns out to nothing, lets grow
beneath each mid-field bush
a perfect shadow, and among
frost-whitened tussocks
the last of night recedes along
tracks the animals have taken
back into earth and wood.

Stand

Andrew Waterman

Coming Down

Our cylinder of hushed steel tilts, slides down;
and lives contracted to the beating of the engines

see startling, iridescent laciness
spread on the waters of the night, lit London:

whorls and radials of orange, blue,
turquoise, an insubstantial rainbow-froth

that might swirl away down its black holes.
Yet flashes stammering there the motivation

of an electric train, and smaller lights
moving, speak of human purposes.

Unreal; till grounded and bussed in, and stood
jostled on hard pavement, a quarrel breaks

behind me: 'I will.' 'You won't.' 'You'll see I will.'
Giving back local scale and weight.

I check my map. Above me, bowed lamps roof
intricacies shutting out the dark waste spaces.

Encounter

Lives of the Poets

Edwin Morgan Notes on one Poet's Working Day

I'm a reader in English at Glasgow University. Glasgow is a big university, and the English classes are large – 450 in the first-year class at the moment[1] (which has to be split into two and the lectures given twice). The Scottish M.A. Honours is a 4-year course, so we have these four classes plus a fifth, called the Advanced, which is an alternative third year course for those who are taking an Ordinary not an Honours degree. So we've these five classes, which involve a mixture of lectures, seminars, and tutorials. This year I'm teaching four out of the five classes. I have five courses of lectures to give, on Medieval Scots poetry, Victorian poetry, Emily Brontë's *Wuthering Heights*, Robert Burns, and James Hogg's *Confessions of a Justified Sinner*. I also have a regular series of seminars on Scottish literature for those who are taking a special optional paper in the final on that subject, and of course I have also some postgraduate students to supervise.

That's the bare bones of the job. It's difficult to describe a typical day because every day is different. Some days are relatively free, with only an hour or two of seminars or tutorials, others are really packed on a 10-till-5 basis. But here's a sample day from earlier this week: – Alarm goes off at 8 o'clock. While I'm having my tea and toast and rice krispies I'm listening to the radio and when I get to the last cup of tea I look through the papers – never quite relaxed because I'm always thinking about what's going to come up during the day and I'm by nature an anxious sort of character. I don't usually have to leave the house till about half past nine. There's generally a good deal of mail and I like to go through this before I leave. This day there's a couple of invoices which I add to a large clip marked DAMNED

1. November 1972.

BILLS; there's an invitation to read my poetry at a school in Dumfriesshire and I spend some time looking up timetables to see how possible it would be to get there; and there is also Part 26 of the *Dictionary of the Older Scottish Tongue*, from Naturall to Nyxttocum, which I know it would be fatal to start dipping into.

I get to the university, partly by bus partly by walking, shortly before 10, collect my mail there, go to my room, and hold an individual tutorial from 10 to 11, discussing with a man in his final year two essays he'd written on Dickens and Tennyson. I have a lecture at 12, on Tennyson – on *Maud*, which I haven't done before, so I look over my notes and make some last-minute changes and additions and make sure I can quickly find the passages I want to read. Also, in this hour before 12, I answer one or two letters, answer the telephone once or twice, and for quarter of an hour go to the staff club for a coffee.

Conversation in club: Did you know our new colleague has arrived? No, what's her name? Heather Glen. You're joking. No it really is Heather Glen; she comes from Australia, via Cambridge. And is she medieval? No no, she's Blake and Wordsworth. But I thought we were short of early Renascence characters? Maybe so, but she's not one. Is she Miss, Mrs, Dr, or what? The answer to this question never emerged – in comes someone waving an old briefcase. Is this what you're looking for Hannah? I don't know, it's so long since I mislaid it, has it got a lock? Yes it's got a lock, and there's a tiny wee key tied on with a bit of string, should we open it? I'm not sure, I'm just not sure, let me feel it, it should have my Pope notes in it. Go on, give it a squeeze Hannah, it won't do it any harm. All right, let's open it. Sorry, the string's not long enough to get the key in, we'll have to cut it. Anybody got a knife or something? Morgan supplies pocket scissors. Oh man, that's a dangerous weapon. It's all right, it's for self defence. Snap. Lock's open. Hannah rummages. Yes, here's old Pope, it's mine. At that moment the university clock chimes out twelve and I scurry off to my lecture.

After the lecture at one o'clock I go to staff club, have lunch, back to my room at 2. For a minute or two I stand looking down into the quadrangle. It's a dark showery day, with gusts of wind, and I watch one of the gardeners trying to sweep up fallen leaves into a sack, letting the wind blow them in as much as he can. Three girls run past, hurrying for a class. Miniskirts under maxicoats, which is always rather eyecatching. The gardener stops and looks up and grins as they fly past. Everything about them is streaming in the wind – their hair, scarves, coats, shoulder-bags – they are like figures in a Japanese print. I wonder if anyone else at some other window is watching me watching the gardener watching the girls. It is all gone in a minute, but is beginning to compose itself into a sort of poetic experience, or the first hint or essence of a poetic experience. I recognize the feeling. But it isn't demanding enough for me to do anything about it there and then. I store the observation away in my mind. If it had been stronger I probably would have tried to write something down, though this is always difficult within the university surroundings and I seldom in fact do it.

Anyway I have other things to do: I have to look over a poem which is to be analysed at a seminar at 4 o'clock (Donne's 'Air and Angels'), and I have to work out a programme for a couple of postgraduate students – I know these things will take me till about 4. So – the seminar on Donne, ending at 5. I have a long wait for a bus, get back home about a quarter to six. A friend comes in at 6 and we have tea; he had been out of work (he's a factory storeman) for more than six months and has just got a new job; we decide to go out and see a film, *The Godfather*, which at least makes a nice contrast to 'Air and Angels'. I get back to the flat al 11 o'clock, make tea, read an essay for a tutorial the following morning (this takes about an hour, as it's a long essay: but it has to be done). Then I take a paperknife and cut the pages of Part 26 of the *D.O.S.T.*, stopping at some of the fascinating words on the way, over a sip of whisky and a nibble of shortbread. Bed about 1 a.m.

In this sort of job, poems usually have to be written either in the evenings or at the weekend or during vacations. You can accommodate to this, you can accommodate to the specific rhythm of the work, though not without tensions and frustrations. The worst part of the job, in a big university like Glasgow, is the marking of essays and exam-papers – even with a substantial staff this is a heavy and soul-battering occupation, and it normally has to be done at home. There's often a real clash between the desire to write poetry and the necessity to get so many papers marked by a certain deadline. And there's no way out of this except by burning the midnight oil. This may not happen frequently, as far as the really large batches of papers are concerned, but it is bad enough, and it is at these moments that you feel like giving up the job. But the moments pass, and I have found – and I can only speak for myself – that with its various disadvantages the job does seem to suit me. I seem to need some tension, some anxiety, some clash of responsibilities, and if I am too free I may be less creative. I don't find the academic life deadening (though I'm sure some people do), partly because I enjoy teaching and partly because I keep a lot of other interests going which are non-academic and even anti-academic. I like to keep a separation between my academic working life and my life outside the university hours. For this reason, being an ordinary member of the English department suits me better, I think, than having a special position as a campus poet, which I have never sought. This is obviously not an argument against having campus writers. But speaking for myself, I would only make the point that it's not impossible to combine an academic job with creative work.

Ambit

Charles Causley A Precise Reticence

I first read, and admired, the poems of William Plomer in the pages of John Lehmann's *New Writing* during the war. Their wit, precision, apparent simplicity, and power (he used words as carefully and exactly as wartime grocers weighed sugar) attracted me, as well as their compelling quietness of tone. Quietness of tone was not a major feature of existence in the hell's kitchen of service life in the second (or any) world war: in my case, on the lower-deck of the Royal Navy.

I also had that remarkable first volume of autobiography *Double Lives*: a salutary piece of writing (particularly on the subject of the Japanese) to read in an aircraft-carrier heading in the uncomfortable direction of the Pacific. This led me, over the next decade or so, to search out everything Plomer had published, whether as poet, novelist, or biographer. Nothing he wrote, it seemed – and seems – to me, lacked distinction. His work has a civilized and civilizing quality, always original and often years ahead of its time. His novel *Turbott Wolfe*, for example, written – amazingly – at the age of eighteen, remains, after half a century, a seminal work on the subject of apartheid.

We didn't meet until about 1962, when I found myself a fellow member of the (then) Arts Council Literature Panel. For most of the meetings, held round a board-room table the shape, size, and appearance of a swimming-bath filled to the brim with gleaming toffee, I was too nervous to say much. Plomer, however, obviously a born committee-member, seemed actually to be enjoying himself. His conversation, like his writing and his personal appearance, was immaculate: never a semi-colon (or a hair) out of place. He spoke quietly and precisely, with a faintly ecclesiastical boom: the voice, perhaps, of a mischievous Archdeacon with a side-line in African magic.

He was always immensely courteous, and the eyes would twinkle with glee at the faintest sign of humour, as well as of pomposity. I was deeply impressed by his fundamental seriousness, his gentleness and kindness, his firmness and common-sense, as well as by the tolerance and understanding he showed his fellow men.

William really liked people – however unlikely they may have seemed – and this was the source and strength of a lot of his work. He read and lectured – a tallish, slight figure, very correctly dressed – with a genuine love for his audience. The less grand it was, and the more humbly it was devoted to literature, the more he seemed to enjoy it. He also saw his own rôle in the proceedings with a pleasant lack of weight. 'I . . . jawed away . . . to a most sympathetic & likeable audience', he once wrote to me in that smooth Japanese hand, '& . . . had the chance of conversation with a good assortment of them. Goodness, how welcoming they were, & how interesting.' On another occasion, when about to set off to the country as President of the Poetry Society for the anniversary dinner of a poetry 'circle', he wrote: 'I shall wear a dinner jacket – it's an antique model, like its owner. They can't all be Homers & Dantes, but they've kept their "circle" going for sixty years, & they read poetry (which, after all, is what it's for) as well as trying to write it, so I shall butter them up a bit.'

His letters almost always had something memorable in them, like some shining bonus of divine green stamps. 'I am going to St. Andrews . . .' he wrote in 1967. 'I always think the Scots are the Zulus of the north.' Odd bits of information, surprising discoveries, always fascinated him. In 1971, he finished up a long letter in which he had been much concerned about a writer ill and in need of financial help, with: 'I've met two different chaps lately who can say – and do say – that they saw Byron "in the flesh". It was when his coffin was opened in the 'thirties. He had been sent home from Greece in a barrel of rum, and, as I needn't remind you, rum does tend to keep one going.'

It was absolutely appropriate that Plomer, with his highly-developed, highly associative sense of the past, resolutely phone-less and, apparently, also typewriter-less, should have moved to an address like Adastra Avenue, Hassocks. I once asked him about it and he replied (November 1970): 'I don't know which is odder, Adastra or Hassocks. The latter means clumps of bushes or tussocks of grass: the former is derived from a local park given by a landowner whose son was killed flying in the '14–'18 War. He wished it to be called Adastra Park, taking the name from the "ad astra" in the motto of the R.F.C.'

He always relished tales of my adventures in junior classrooms during twenty-six years of teaching ('that's a proper life's work, far grander than my nearly forty years as a part-time publisher's reader'), and one could sense his instinctive sympathy with and understanding of children. 'I've just been reading,' he wrote me last year, 'about a boy with strict and I think cruel Evangelical relations who shut him up for hours alone (about 1840) in a medieval chapel in Sussex . . . with two life-size recumbent figures in armour, no lights (in the boy's time), and rats about. They took away his cat & hanged it for no reason except that he was very fond of it, & they thought he needed, or pretended they thought he needed, to be deprived of pleasure of any kind. Not a good story to tell a convalescent – but I like to think of your sympathy with the child.'

I once asked him gloomily, over a drink, if he thought it a good idea to accept a commission to write a poem on a set theme, or for a particular occasion. I'd forgotten, of course, that he was one of the very few poets who could bring off a 'public' poem of this kind and make it, at the same time, a distinctively personal piece. (*The Planes of Bedford Square*, which he wrote for the Book Bang in 1971, illustrates this.) His response was immediate. 'Certainly,' he said. 'Remember, the people who commission a poem don't expect a masterpiece. It's a useful exercise for the poet. There's just the possibility that the poem might really come off – one never knows. And there's always the money.'

Although basically a quiet man, and a remarkably good listener, William could be a formidable monologuist when the rare occasion arose. In 1966, we took part in a 'conversation' recorded by the Central Office of Information for distribution abroad. The subject was Poets' Corner. We'd met in the Abbey, earlier in the day, and had been wandering vaguely about trying to work out who was there, and – more important, perhaps – who wasn't. I was a little apprehensive about my ability to keep the double-act going during the recording, but I needn't have worried. William was magnificent. 'Hello!' the recording-engineer said to me cheerfully as we emerged from the studio. 'I thought you'd gone home.'

The last time I saw him was in April of this year, when we read, together with Ted Hughes, in Wales. I remember William's uninhibited delight at the splendidly unimpressed comment on our performance as reported from a member of the audience: 'A bunch of amateurs. They didn't even know their own words. *Reading from books!*'

There was nothing amateur, as a human being or as a writer, about William Plomer. His work, always distinguished, ranged from the huge themes of Africa to the death, in a Sussex garden, of a hedge-sparrow. (Almost the last poem in his last collection, *Celebrations*.)

To mind there sprang
A Roman phrase, *Ubi humilitas,*
Ibi majestas. Great marble word
For an almost weightless corpse!
My little pang was not excess
Of sentiment, it was proportionate
(Sole witness, I affirm) to what I saw.

He once quoted to me something said by Wei T'ai in the eleventh century: 'Poetry presents the thing in order to convey the feeling. It should be precise about the thing and reticent about the feeling, for as soon as the mind responds and connects with the thing the feeling shows in the words; this is how poetry enters deeply into us.' It seems to me the perfect comment on the work, and the life, of William Plomer.

London Magazine

Among the back files of our school magazine at Wellington Girls' College was an early issue containing a little story by Kathleen Beauchamp, aged ten: this was Katherine Mansfield's first published work. Two of the houses in which she had lived in the late 1890s were within a few minutes' walk of the school. It didn't seem to me or my friends that writing was an unusual occupation for a woman.

I myself inclined to verse rather than fiction in my teens (although I had an adventure-serial running in the children's page of the evening newspaper for some time). But here again there were precedents: among the New Zealand poems we studied was 'The Long Harbour', by Ursula Bethell. It's a school-anthology piece, well-wrought but too romantic for my present taste; but her shorter, less formal poems are more sympathetic and still have something to say to me. Then there was Robin Hyde (born Iris Wilkinson), who wrote novels and poetry, travelled through the battlefields of China in the 1930s, and died (we thought) an enviably tragic death in London.

I wasn't crazy about Katherine Mansfield, Ursula Bethell or Robin Hyde when I was at school. I had other literary heroes, and the poems I knew by heart tended to be older than theirs (Donne, Shakespeare, Goethe, Blake appealed to me). But these three women were writers from my own country, quite recently dead, and part of an accepted tradition; it was somehow mildly comforting to have them in the background and to know that eccentric though I might be – and I hoped at least that I was that – writing poetry wasn't a desperately outlandish ambition for a girl.

Looking further back into literary history I found fewer women poets. In the nineteenth century there were the two Emilys – the tormented passionate Brontë striding over her bleak moors, and the little white caged bird in New England, Emily Dickinson: each in her own way outside convention, each clearly odd. And of course there were Christina Rossetti and Elizabeth Barrett Browning. Behind them lay long centuries of almost entirely male territory, relieved only by occasional female names – Aphra Behn, Anne Countess of Winchelsea, Vittoria Colonna, Moero of Byzantium, and, right back there at the start, Sappho.

It has become boring to wonder why, to analyse the reasons (most of which we more or less understand by now) for male predominance in the arts. The point is that in literature at least it's now over. As novelists women came to the top long ago, and as poets they've been comfortably at home up there for forty years or more. Two of the best American poets of this century are Marianne Moore and Elizabeth Bishop; in Britain we've had, among others, Stevie Smith; and, claimed by both countries and divided unhappily between them, Sylvia Plath. These are all brilliant writers, in quite different ways, and none could be accused of being preoccupied with feminine concerns: Marianne Moore wrote about practically anything one could think of – animals and insects, music, architecture, medical research and baseball; her glittering multi-faceted poems are mosaics made up of an incredibly wide range of materials; and as a technical innovator (if she didn't invent the syllabic form she certainly remade it) she has been enormously influential.

Elizabeth Bishop is also a highly-skilled craftsman. She is acutely visual – her scenes leap before the eyes – but at the same time a metaphysician, a player with ideas; and there is a warmth and human immediacy to her writing; humour, too – some of her poems about Brazil have made me laugh aloud with delight.

Dear Stevie Smith, who died in 1971, was quite another kind of creature: utterly original, completely independent of literary fashions – her sad, funny, quirky verses give no sign that she ever read anything apart from Edward Lear and Hymns Ancient and Modern. She looked and talked like an English lady, which indubitably she was; but her knights and princesses, her lonely young dreamers and dead babies, her cats and dogs and jungle-dwellers speak with a variety of other voices.

One could go on: about Sylvia Plath, for example (but I think the time has come for a temporary lull in goings-on about Sylvia Plath, much as I admire her work); about good, competent, interesting British poets like Patricia Beer; or about European and Russian women poets, and the rest. There they all are; I have named only a few favourites.

There is no question, then, that women can be poets in the fullest sense: they have proved that they can. This is not to say, though, that there is no discrimination, no talk by critics and reviewers of 'feminine sensibility' and the like; and such phrases are not confined to those whose imagination is weak. Douglas Dunn, an intelligent critic and a poet himself, expressed a widely-held view when he wrote recently 'The nature of their perceptions . . . is peculiarly different from the masculine standard, as if eyes had gender'. Quite possibly he's right: as a member of only one sex I don't feel qualified to judge. But we are not after all trying to pretend that we are not women. Critics write also of black poets, Jewish poets, Marxist poets, and the members of these groups do not or should not object to being characterized, for certain limited purposes, by their origins or allegiances. One is affected by all the circumstances of one's life, and writes out of them. Poets more than most writers tend to use personal material and to 'give themselves away' in their work even when they are not being overtly confessional.

In this connection there is a kindly convention – often more of a convenient fiction – known as 'the persona of the poet' and similar phrases; a critic will politely say 'The character speaking in this poem is a woman recovering from a suicide attempt' rather than 'Miss X is here describing her feelings after attempting suicide'. It doesn't always convince, of course – I knew a poet in New Zealand who was forever appearing at his friends' houses to use their typewriters because if he typed his love-poems in his own study his wife was liable to lean over his shoulder and ask 'Who's that about?' The examination of personal pronouns, incidentally, can be an interesting exercise for the literary news-hound who puts biography before aesthetic considerations, noting for example the use of 'you' and of neutral, genderless words like 'person' and 'being' in the work of homosexual poets too shy to say 'he' and too honest to say 'she' of their lovers.

I've been guilty of similar evasions myself. When I was twenty I wrote a poem about a romantic loner who fell in love with trees and rivers: myself, of course; but out of some half-formed wish to avoid public scrutiny of my character I used the pronoun 'he' throughout – rather transparently, I thought. The result was that people assumed the poem to be about my husband, and his embarrassment was added to my own. With the increased confidence of age and experience I've learnt to do without such devices. The danger in one's thirties is not that of exposing one's thoughts and feelings to the casual reader (they are not, after all, unique or even exceptional thoughts and feelings: they contain few surprises) but of embarrassing one's children by doing so – just as formerly one had to face the possibility of shocking one's grandparents. Women are still perhaps more vulnerable than men to charges of scandalizing members of their families.

But these are trivial considerations: they might

temporarily prevent a poet from publishing certain material but not, if the impulse is strong enough, from writing it. The serious problems now for male and female poets alike are those common to all artists – questions of priorities, of divided loyalties, of such basic elements as time, money and way of life. Almost any poet has to decide over and over again whether it is more important to finish a poem or to spend some time with his children or friends; whether he is justified in neglecting his job to scribble down a few words which are obsessing him; whether in fact he ought to have a job at all – would it not be more honest and more satisfying to go freelance, or to work for wages only when the bills pile up? But in that case might his family not suffer? All writers have their own variations on such dilemmas, and sex has nowadays very little to do with it; among my friends male poets and female novelists share with me the same difficulties. The problem is less that of writer as woman than that of writer as social being with conflicting responsibilities – which, unlike the status of women, cannot be expected to alter much. We must be grateful for the work of our predecessors, and continue to get on with the job as best we can ourselves.

Books N.B.L.

Anthony Thwaite A Few Memories: In Homage

Between the ages of fifteen and seventeen, I seem to have composed several letters of homage and/or sheer impertinence to living poets who had momentarily taken my fancy. I wrote to T. S. Eliot concerning my doubts about Christianity: he did not reply. I wrote to C. Day Lewis to confirm my conviction that the way of Dylan Thomas was the only hope for poetry: he replied courteously and charmingly, and I now wonder why I didn't have the cheek to write to Thomas himself. I wrote to Henry Treece, enclosing a critical essay on his work, on which he commented that he was grateful for the flattering things I had said but preferred old English sheepdogs to poets.

But these letters and the opinions they carried were only sudden impulses. My true homage was to George Barker. I suppose I must have first read his poems in Michael Roberts's *Faber Book of Modern Verse* and Yeats's Oxford anthology, but I know that the first book of his I bought was *Calamiterror*, in a Birmingham bookshop visited when changing trains on the way back to boarding school in Bath. I was sixteen. Immediately I knew that my pantheon of Langland, Blake and Dylan Thomas would have to be extended. For a long time after that it was a bad week if I hadn't written six poems, and all of them rolled and reverberated with Barkerian rhetoric.

Being the school poet was a heady but frustrating job. I was steered away from my ambition to edit the school literary magazine, *Piazza*, by schoolmasters who averred that it would interfere with my Latin, though I still think the real reason was they supposed it would make me more swollen-headed than I was already. The next best thing was to contribute copiously to the magazine, which I did. My efforts included a poem called 'Variation on a Theme by George Barker', which took a line from *Calamiterror* and descanted on it. When *Piazza* was printed, I slipped a copy of it into an envelope, along with sundry other poems of mine, and sent it to this unknown but hallowed George Barker c/o Faber & Faber.

The response was all I could have hoped. A thin foreign-feeling envelope arrived from the south of France, addressed to me in spiky Elizabethan handwriting. Mr. Barker liked my poem; he advised me to keep my singing robes well laundered; to my absurd question, 'Am I a poet, do you think I am any good?' he opined that it was really a matter of 'For God's sake stop or for God's sake go on'; and that he supposed I was young. He also wrote that, since my Muse appeared to have more mandrake than man in her, he suggested I use blood.

I thirsted for such assurances, such apophthegms. A few loyal friends were shown the letter, and were impressed, and before long I had packed up an even larger envelope and sent its load of verses to George Barker. This time the reply came from London. It confirmed the earlier remarks about being a poet, and went on to say: 'The poet is a scapegoat disguised as a scrapegrace. See to it that you acquire the grace to escape from'. Most head-turning of all, the letter ended: 'If you are ever in London, why not come and break salt with me or whatever the hell it is one breaks'.

My inclination was to leap on the next London train and make straight for Stanhope Gardens, S.W.7. But it was term time, Somerset was a long way from London, and in any case I spent the holidays in Leicester with my parents. I hardly knew London at all, and couldn't imagine when I might go there. But then, fortuitously, my father's job was moved to Muswell Hill: the literary mysteries of the capital were about to be revealed to me. The next holidays – of Christmas 1947 – I arrived in

South Kensington with an A–Z street-guide and presented myself at the Barker doorstep.

He was not there; he was round the corner mending a car with his brother Kit. So my first view of the legendary poet was of a well-sculpted but greased face peering out from under the chassis of a large, battered but powerful vehicle. I announced myself. 'At last', he said, and as far as I was concerned all became a blur. I remember little of whatever else happened that afternoon, except that I think we visited an exhibition at the Victoria & Albert. But he looked and sounded and behaved exactly as a poet should.

And that was and is his importance to me, quite apart from the value of the poetry itself. During the eighteen months or so that followed, I saw George Barker a few times: I remember one meeting in particular, in the Black Horse in Rathbone Place, just off Oxford Street, when I drank an unaccustomed quantity of bitter and heard him speak the astounding words, 'I'll show your poems to Eliot, if you like, and see whether he wants them for Faber'. Whether the offer was ever taken up, and, if it was, what Eliot thought of them, I don't know. But the kindness, the amused seriousness, the refusal to reduce this naïve, pert, opinionated, baby-faced public schoolboy to pulp (which he could so easily have done) have always stayed with me. Later, when I left school and had to do my army service, I wrote to George Barker from Winchester and Bodmin and various garrisons in Libya, and had from him some well-chosen mantic epigrams and advice (such as that, if I were going to hand-print a booklet of my poems – an idea that came to nothing – I should somehow acquire a font of Bodoni, because it had the proper shape for poems). Some of the letters were written in that characteristic hand, others were typed with generous triple-spacing onto a brown ribbon I have never seen anywhere else. They all had what someone has called *une nature riche*.

He came to Oxford when I was an undergraduate there, and at my invitation read his poems to the university poetry society, drinking with only a few aspersions the foul British-type sherry we provided and swaying down my spiral staircase with the remark, 'My dear Thwaite, you cost too much'. After Oxford, my wife and I visited him on our honeymoon, slopping down a muddy cart-track somewhere near Haslemere and finding him in a woodcutter's cottage with no running water. We were about to sail for Japan, where I was to take up my first job teaching at Tokyo University. Of his own experiences at Sendai in 1940, he told us that he was followed everywhere by a tiny spy in white gloves, and that the calligraphy was upsetting. This was challenging, though I discovered that my own feelings were different about 'the island where/The soul is shallower than a bowl of tea/And negative as water'. But of course he was there at a particularly bad time.

There have been long periods between 1947 and today when I haven't been in touch with George Barker, haven't even known whether he was in Italy or Islington, Norfolk or Nevada. But he has been a presence, a type, an example at the back of my consciousness of what a poet's calling is. As a radio producer and editor, I broadcast and published him, but always with the suspicion that the true poet is not a go-between or cultural functionary. I suppose that what I am saying is that I still have Romantic aspirations towards some imagined ideal of the poet – aspirations that may seem belied by the kind of poetry I have written myself and the kind of professional life I have led; and that such an ideal is embodied in George Barker.

I have suddenly realized that I am now eight years older than George Barker was when, in my guise of what he once called 'AngelThwace', I first met him under that car in South Kensington. It's a chastening thought. To have achieved what he has done in the best of his poems, without compromises and solely devoted to his art, is an example to the less single-minded of us. He will continue to be an example, long after the age of sixty.

Homage to George Barker, Brian & O'Keeffe

> And in your verses remembre to place every worde in his natural *Emphasis* or sound, that is to say in such wise, and with such length or shortnesse, elevation or depression of sillables, as it is commonly pronounced or used.
>
> George Gascoigne: *Certayne notes of Instruction concerning the making of verse or ryme in English.*

The best definition of poetry, for me, has been Dryden's: 'articulate music'. I also see a poem as sculpture – a shape implicit in language, like a statue in a block of marble.

The form of a poem is primarily aural. So long as we live in the era of the printed word its aspect on the page is important. But less important than the images that the words of the poem convey; these are part of its form, like the emotions or emotion that the poem evokes or refers to.

To make a poem is to sculpt an aural form which will communicate something seen, experienced, felt, and/or thought. A poem is the best, i.e. most efficient mode of communicating a complex, of simultaneously presenting the various factors. Cf. Pound's image of poetry as a centaur – 'the thinking word-arranging, clarifying faculty must move and leap with the energizing, sentient, musical faculties'. And his afterthought: 'I dare say there are very good marksmen who just can't shoot from a horse.'

So much for general considerations. To turn to the particular, I am in the disadvantageous position of not being able, except in what must be classed as imagination, to hear the aural forms that ask to be made.[1] Many words in my vocabulary I have never

1. David Wright has been completely deaf since the age of seven (ed.).

heard pronounced, or even seen spoken. Yet it's not likely that MacDiarmid picked up all the material of his magnificently orchestrated opening sentence to *On a Raised Beach* by ear:

> All is lithogenesis – or lochia,
> Carpolite fruit of the forbidden tree,
> Stones blacker than any in the Caaba,
> Cream-coloured caen-stone, chatoyant pieces,
> Celadon and corbeau, bistre and beige,
> Glaucous, hoar, enfouldered, cyathiform,
> Making mere faculae of the sun and moon,
> I study you glout and gloss, but have
> No cadrans to adjust you with, but turn again
> From optik to haptik and like a blind man run
> My fingers over you, arris by arris, burr by burr,
> Slickensides, truité, rugas, foveoles,
> Bringing my aesthesia in vain to bear,
> An angle-titch to all your corrugations and coigns,
> Hatched foraminous cavo-rilieva of the world,
> Diectic, fiducial stones, Chiliad by chiliad
> What bricole piled you here, stupendous cairn?

Subject to correction, I'd venture that much of this vocabulary was visually got, out of a dictionary or geological treatise.

But in my own case what bothers me is frequent uncertainty where stress or accent properly falls. In my early days I used to go in for free-ranging exercises in what I thought was sprung rhythm. Too many lines, stanzas, or what might be called verbal sonatinas, got spoiled by mistakes in accentuation. Though it is of course possible to make a word or syllable bear stress that it doesn't naturally carry. Good effects are to be obtained thus – but it must be done with the eyes, or rather the ears, open, the poet being aware of what he's up to. Accidental felicities of this type are rare, and mostly devalued by a surround of accidental infelicities.

Back in 1949, about the time of the publication of my first book failed sprung verse, I began tackling this problem. A poem needs a frame as much as a picture – a defined area in which it is to operate. Metric provides this frame. Stanza-forms, rhyme-schemes, arbitrary forms like the sonnet, do not constrain or confine so much as compress and focus, just as you obtain power from steam by restricting its field of expansion. Requiring a frame of which I could be certain, i.e. independent of any fallibility in the matter of 'natural *Emphasis*', I decided on a mathematical one – my verse would be contained by a count of syllables rather that of accents or stresses, though I did not entirely discard the latter. I'd never heard of syllabic verse, which so far as I remember did not come into fashion till the mid-fifties or thereabouts. Mine wasn't – I should say isn't – orthodox syllabic verse and did not set out to be. It was a way of providing a frame for the aural forms I was trying to elicit. A more or less arbitrary count of syllables – say nine, or eleven, or twelve, or thirteen to the line – into which I have to fit the beat, or rhythmic imperative, called for by the poem. I seldom if ever use a line of ten syllables because of the ease with which it slips into an iambic pentameter beat, resonant of too much familiar English verse.

Rhyme of a sort, as part of the frame needed for the aural form, and attendant rhyme-schemes to be more or less strictly adhered to, is also necessary to my system. Full rhymes I find too heavy, too familiar to the ear – aurally hackneyed so to speak – to use much except on special occasions. So I go for half-rhymes, ear-rhymes, vowel-rhymes, consonant-rhymes, and a peculiar not to say idiosyncratic form of eye-rhyming. It took me some time to realize the principle behind the latter – to find out why these eye-rhymes "worked". I was not using words of similar spelling but different pronunciation ('though' and 'through' and so on) but homophones, lip-reader's rhymes in fact. For example this stanza rhyming abab:

> No I am not speaking of professional bohemians
> Of those who mine for status in the stratas of
>   culture;
> I mean those who are not in the service of a
>   competence
> But of an extraneous vision, of an idea.

Very little that's useful – for a practising poet anyway – seems to have been written about English prosody, apart from Campion's *Observations in the Art of English Poesy*, Coleridge's preface to *Christabel*, Coventry Patmore's *Essay on English Prosody*, Hopkins's preface to his own poems, and an extraordinarily interesting but little-known article by Professor David Abercrombie, *A Phonetician's View of Verse Structure*,[1] which points out that it is a special way of organizing the sound-producing movements, rather than the sound of speech itself, that results in verse ('All rhythm, it seems likely, is ultimately rhythm of bodily movement'). A year or two ago I saw some very intriguing and apposite remarks on the subject by John Wain, in some review that he wrote for the *Observer*; but I lost the cutting; I wish he would expand his ideas into an essay.

A point that fascinates me, one which I have been unable to investigate for the same reason that enabled me to note it, is the inexplicable quality of poetry that allows it to communicate its verbal music in different or even unauthentic pronunciations. Alexander Pope did not pronounce English as we know it; Shakespeare's vowel-sounds were not ours; Chaucer reading *The Canterbury Tales* would be unintelligible. Yet the sound-effects of their verse

1. Published in *Linguistics*, June 1964.

seem unimpaired by modern pronunciation. And there is the point that the auditory qualities of the poetry of Homer and Virgil come through to us though Latin and Greek are dead languages and no one exactly knows how they were spoken.

The analogy may be that a tune played on the piano can be recognizable when rendered on a penny whistle.

When I begin a poem I have at back of my consciousness a rhythm – a sound-pattern? – a music? – for which I have to cast a frame (a syllabic count for the verse, a rhyming order of one kind or another) and find for it words that fit, recreate, or express, that rhythm, sound-pattern, or music.

George Barker once described this initial process of making a poem:

'It's like listening to a long-distance telephone call on a bad line.'

Agenda